Risking It
An Intersection of Faith & Work

A Memoir by Tim Hoerr
With Alyssa Kolb

Copyright © 2015

Published by Serra Creative, a division of Serra Ventures, LLC

Copyright © 2015 by Timothy C. Hoerr.

All rights reserved.

Published by Serra Creative, a division of Serra Ventures, LLC

ISBN 978-0692282458

All photos by Alyssa Kolb. Copyright © 2015. All rights reserved.

Designed by Pat Mayer

No part of this publication may be reproduced, stored in a retrieval system or transmitted in any form or by any means, electronic, mechanical, photocopying, recording, scanning or otherwise, except as permitted under Section 107 or 108 of the 1976 United States Copyright Act, without the prior written permission of Serra Ventures, LLC. Requests for permission should be addressed to Timothy C. Hoerr, CEO, Serra Ventures, LLC, 2021 South First Street, Suite 206, Champaign, Illinois 61820, 217.819.5200, fax 217.819.5205, email info@serraventures.com.

*To Toni, Alyssa & Nate, Audra & Eric and Kaley
You've made the journey so joyful and rich!*

Table of Contents

Prologue 1

Part 1—Roots

1. Joining Dad in the Work He was Doing 4
2. Seeds of Faith 8
3. Seeds of Entrepreneurship 14
4. Pearls in the Poop 18
5. A God Encounter at Turkey Run 21
6. Real Freedom 25
7. Set Apart 29
8. It Added Up 34
9. A Redbird Spreads His Wings 38
10. Big City Kid 44
11. Called 50
12. Cracking the Code to Become a Leader 59
13. Czech Mate—New Game 66

Part 2—Risking It

14. Go West, Young Man! 74
15. Teamwork 82
16. Thank God It's Monday! 87
17. A Setup for Success? Not. 94
18. In the Rearview Mirror 101
19. Just Do It 105
20. All That Glitters? 111
21. A Temporary Stopover 117
22. 20/20 Vision 124
23. Have You Seen the Lyt? 129
24. Rest 135
25. The Best Sammich I Ever Had 142

Part 3—Relationships

26.	You Reap What You Sow	150
27.	Breaking Up Is Hard to Do	155
28.	Sail On	162
29.	A Day (20 Years, Actually) at the Beach	167
30.	Kaley's Dilemma	173
31.	Tuesday Morning Coffee Break	181
32.	Mark Shannon—A Brilliant Flame Gone Too Soon	185
33.	Worship, Pray, Give	190

Part 4—Reflections

34.	Inflection Points	198
35.	Like Good Wine, Most Things in Life Take (a Long) Time	207
36.	Touching God	214
37.	God's Bigger Story (and How Yours Fits In)	221

Acknowledgements	227
About the Authors	229

Prologue

A long series of tables in the large fellowship hall of the Apostolic Christian Church in Peoria, Illinois were lined end to end, laden with an assortment of fried chicken, meatloaf, deviled eggs, tapioca salad, baked beans, fresh fruit salad, and probably a hundred other potluck dishes. I was five or six years old, and the annual Sunday School picnic, held in June, was a not-to-be-missed affair. In addition to the bountiful spread of homemade food (most potlucks these days seem to feature store-bought potato salad, Doritos, relish trays from the deli, and Oreos), there were gunny sack races, water balloon tosses, and the Sunday School superintendent with his helpers handing out little ice cream cups with wooden spoons attached. All of this occurred in a rather pastoral setting—large, grassy expanses; a playground complete with swings and teeter-totters; an abundance of mature shade trees—and an inviting five-acre pond.

After dinner, along with my cousin, Jeff, I'd wandered down to the edge of the pond. Today's doting parents are likely horrified of the thought of a youngster wandering around on his own, let alone the fact that I was exploring an alluring body of water. The long, dry grass of the lawn was met by the muddy bank of the water. A variety of cattails and reeds grew just beyond the bank. I remember the day as warm and humid, the early evening sun still shining brightly.

Just that month, I had heard the story of Jesus walking on the water in the middle of a tumultuous storm as related in the New Testament, the Book of Matthew, Chapter 14. I was admittedly quite intrigued by the powerful image of Jesus—and then Peter—walking on the surface of the water amidst a raging rainstorm. It seemed quite fantastical—and yet very real. I'm fairly certain that I hadn't developed the appropriate discretion to know whether this story and my own life experience somehow meshed.

The thought occurred to me then—and is one I've continued to ask in a metaphoric sense over the course of fifty years or so—if I step out onto the water, might not something awesome and wonderful happen? Something out of the ordinary?

"If Jesus could do it, why can't I do it?" I asked Jeff.

"Are you serious?" Jeff gasped, wide-eyed. "I don't know about this."

"Sure, why not? What's the worst that could happen?"

I proceeded to step with full force onto the water, expecting the surface to somehow firm up beneath my shoes. Instead, I fell headlong into the surrounding reeds with a resounding SPLASH! Jeff reached for me and yanked me by my right arm back to safety. Fortunately, the water was only a foot or two deep at that point. My clothes were soaked, my tennis shoes caked with mud. Yet I recall a big grin on my face. I also remember thinking that my parents would not be amused.

I had learned a poignant lesson on risk that day. One that most of us learn quite early in life. A lesson on risk-taking that, for many of us, tends to be reinforced time and again. Indeed, this lesson defined and constrained the first half of my life or so.

The lesson, simply stated, is this: Risking it can be dangerous. Risking it might cause unexpected results. In risking it, you might just end up all wet.

PART 1

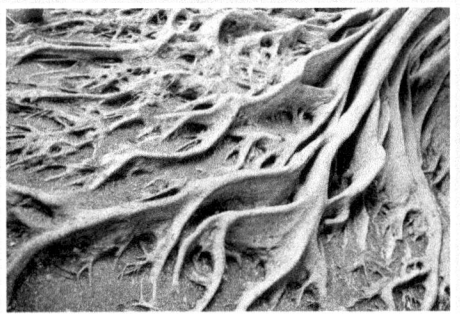

Roots

It's been said that in order to gain proper perspective on the present (and future), we would do well to examine and understand the past. This first section explores some of the foundational experiences of my youth and young adulthood. These are stories that represent poignant memories—incidents and circumstances that proved to be powerful shaping experiences in my life.

1. Joining Dad in the Work He's Doing

Peoria, Illinois
August 1970

I FINISHED MY LAST BIT OF RHUBARB PIE while sitting at our family's kitchen table. Then I licked my lips clean of a few bits of lingering crust. As a nine-year-old, I didn't want to waste any pie. My younger brother Nate and older brother Ben were just finishing their pieces as well.

"That pie was awesome, Mom!" I said.

"I'm glad you enjoyed it, Timmy. Do you want another piece?" Mom asked as she cleared the dinner dishes.

"No thanks. I'm stuffed."

"How about you boys?" she said to Nate and Ben.

"Nah, I'm full too," Ben said.

"All right. Can you bring your plates and glasses over to the sink for me?"

I could see Nate was pondering whether he could stuff anymore pie into his gullet when my dad walked into the kitchen.

"Hey boys, I've got to head over to the Caterpillar Mossville plant tonight to check up on a landscape we installed there today. Make sure they're watering the new sod and keeping the trees alive. What say you guys join me?" Dad said with a smile.

"I'm in!" I said, quickly clearing my plate and wiping my hands on my pants. "Let's go!"

In my preteen years of 6 to 12, I eagerly looked forward to the evening hours after dinner. My father, who would come home from an exhausting, physically demanding work day around 6 or so, would often have a project or two that needed attention following dinner. And the cool part was my two brothers and I would typically be offered the opportunity to join Dad on these post-dinner excursions. An evening project might involve driving to a new job site to see how the work had progressed that day; or it might mean returning to the garden center/office to prepare an estimate for a new opportunity; or it might consist of moving sprinklers around on a customer's recently-sodded lawn. Though customers were responsible for their own lawns once installed, my dad assured me that we would be replacing the sod at our expense if the customer neglected to water it sufficiently. Dad's practical wisdom (though I don't recall thinking of it as such at the time) became the basis upon which I later built my approach to business.

"All right boys, let's go."

"Ben, are you coming with?" I asked, hoping he'd say yes.

"Not tonight. Got a phone call or two I need to make," Ben said, winking. He seemed to be quite taken with girls, being five years my senior.

Nate and I sprinted to the garage, where dad's Ford pickup was parked. Painted forest green, with a company name and logo emblazoned on each door, a number 6 call-number hand-painted on the driver's side, and the usual assortment of tools, supplies, and such in the rear bed, the truck was a source of pride for me. With the Hoerr Nursery's fleet of over 50 vehicles, the business was well known throughout Peoria, Illinois. More importantly, our reputation for honesty, top-notch service, and unparalleled creativity in meeting customers' needs had made the family business a success for decades, dating back to its founding in 1926 by my grandfather, David August Hoerr.

"Hey, I got the middle seat last time, Nate. You take it this time," I protested as Nate refused to get in before me.

"I had the middle seat on the way to Thompson's with Mom this afternoon. You take it," Nate said.

I groused a bit, but upon agreeing that he would take the middle seat on the way home, I got in. As I slid into my seat, I took in the familiar aromas of leather, oil, dirt, perspiration, and plant foliage. I loved those smells, and there was great comfort being in that old cab—a sense of purpose and place and "being with." Elsewhere, I might be prone to worry about an upcoming test or the neighborhood bully. But not here. Here there was safety, security, and significance all rolled into one.

"We're almost there, boys. See that set of sprinklers running in the distance?"

"Yep. Wow. This is a big job, Dad. Did you do all of this yourself?" I asked.

"Oh, no, Timmy. This is a large commercial job that has had a crew of ten working on it for the last two weeks."

Dad pulled the pickup to the curb, turned off the engine, and jumped out. He moved swiftly to the first sprinkler, about 20 feet away. Repositioning it, he quickly moved on to the next sprinkler, and then the next. Nate and I were running to keep up with him, not seeing any discernable pattern to his movements, but understanding that he certainly knew what he was doing. Within 30 minutes, Dad had completely rearranged all of the sprinklers, and stepped back to survey the site. All seemed to be in order.

"Ok, boys, let's go. We're done for the night."

We hopped back in the cab and I elbowed Nate to cue him for his line. I had asked the last trip out.

"Can we stop at Emo's on the way home, Dad?" Nate asked. Emo's Dairy Dream, with the big clown face, was a summer hot spot, and one of our favorite destinations as youngsters.

"Well, I don't know. Didn't we just have dinner and dessert?"

More elbowing and a suggestive glance between brothers.

"An ice cream cone just sounds good," Nate suggested.

I gave Nate a nod of approval. "Yeah, Dad, an ice cream cone would be a great way to end our day!"

Now it was up to dad. I figured we had a fifty-fifty chance at best.

But stop at Emo's indeed we did. A chocolate dipped cone awaited.

These mini work adventures were perhaps my fondest memories of my times with Dad. In fact, they represented about the only time with him that I can recall other than summertime family vacations. To be with Dad meant to join him in the work he was doing.

Then, of course, I saw no spiritual ties to that statement; it was just material fact. Now, however, I see spiritual truth behind that seemingly simple statement. My father was THE authority figure in my life. I loved him, knew he loved me, and knew he wanted only the best for me. I wanted to grow up to be like him: wise, hard-working, good, and successful. Who wouldn't want to be like that? And so, because he was busy, and adults of that era seemingly had less time than do adults of this era, in spending time with their kids, I entered into his world: the world of work.

It reminds me more than a bit, now, of what Jesus said in John 5:19-20 about the Son being able to do nothing on his own; he can only do what he sees the Father doing, and whatever the Father does, the Son also does. For the Father loves the Son, and shows him all he does. (Talk about the perfect Father-Son relationship!)

As such, my own father was showing me the work he was doing, and I was taking it all in, learning moment by moment and day by day. Through his work, my dad was doing something meaningful—providing beautiful landscapes—with a genuine attitude of serving others and a commitment to excellence. My dad's work seemed to be vitally connected to his faith—they were intertwined, you might say. And so I've found, as I've moved along in life, that I've followed my earthly father in his entrepreneurial bent, all the while attempting to integrate my work with my faith. The two have always been vitally connected for me. Perhaps another way to say it is that through my everyday, work-a-day plans and activities, I've endeavored to join with my heavenly Father in what he is doing.

2. Seeds of Faith

Peoria, Illinois
December, 1973

IN THE FAMILY ROOM FIREPLACE, surrounded by a hearth made of hand-laid brick salvaged from old Peoria buildings, a crackling fire was going. The multicolored lights on the Christmas tree blinked on and off, reflecting off the hodge-podge collection of ornaments and tinsel. The stereo was playing an Andy Williams Christmas album, and Mom had just served hot cider and cut-out cookies to us "worker elves." But this wasn't Santa's toy shop. It looked more like a modern-day Fed Ex Office with about 20 piles of paper, each a couple hundred sheets deep, arranged in a large oval around the supper table. A separate card table had been set up as an envelope stuffing station, and on the floor, boxes were ready to accept the stuffed and stamped envelopes in advance of their imminent trip to the post office.

What were we doing? We were having an "Apostolic Christian World Relief" work party, organized by my dad, the national secretary for the church's humanitarian relief group, and his able assistant, my mother. My brothers and I were the conscripted labor, compensated with Christmas goodies and the satisfaction of supporting a larger cause of which we knew little. This was a ritual we'd come to expect at least once a year, sometimes more often.

"Okay, boys. We're going to run an assembly line here," my dad said. "Starting at this stack, you pick up a page and move to the next stack. Add that page to the one you already have in your hand, and keep moving around the table until you've put all 20 pages together. Make sense?"

"Uh, what happens if I get one of the pages out of order?" I asked.

"We need to do this right, Tim," Dad said, a serious expression on his face. "These are the minutes and reports of the national World Relief organization for our church. It's important that we do this job well, so that all of the churches across the country get the information in proper order. The better job we do tonight, the better people throughout the country will know about the work of World Relief and the importance of stepping up to personally support it."

"Got it. What about doubles? Is it okay if I happen to pick up two pages instead of one, by mistake?" I was feeling rather ornery that evening.

"Ok, smarty pants. Enough of your questions. No, it is not okay to have doubles, either. And if you see a blank sheet in there somewhere—it does happen every now and then—throw that out. Tim and Ben, you are the collators. Mom, you're the envelope stuffer. Nate, you put on the stamps and place the envelopes in the postal boxes. Everyone set?"

And so the assembly line began. Ben, my dad, and I walked around the table, picking up sheets of paper and collating them into sets, tapping the sets on the edge of the table to straighten them, then handing them to my mother, sitting at the card table, for the next step in the operation. After folding, she inserted them into envelopes that she had hand-addressed earlier that afternoon. Once stuffed, she handed them to Nate for stamping and sealing, then placing in one of the postal boxes. Nate, being the youngest of the bunch, was quickly failing behind.

About 30 minutes in, my brothers and I got the picture that this would be an all-night affair. Whatever alternative plans we may have had for the evening (reading a comic book, playing a board game, or working a puzzle—we didn't have a television!), we now understood would be postponed until the next evening. Just what was this World Relief thing, anyway? And why was it so important to support humanitarian aid projects halfway around the world in India and China? How did it make sense to give away time, energy, and money to something so distant, so removed from 6140 Evergreen Circle, Peoria, Illinois? It didn't seem to make sense to me. My world was pretty darn small, you might say.

Besides his commitment to excellence in business and his tireless work ethic, Dad was a man of deep faith. That faith motivated him to action in any number of ways. Although I would characterize most of those actions as very personal—subtle and unassuming, you might say—there was an occasional public face to his faith. The most obvious manifestation was his role as a lay minister in the Apostolic Christian Church and his position as the national secretary of the church's World Relief humanitarian aid organization. In these roles, others observed a public portrayal of what our family saw in private. Reflecting back, the public manifestation matched the private in nearly every respect. Something I took for granted, really—not understanding until older that this is often not the case. My dad was the same guy at home, as leader of his business, and in the pulpit on Sunday mornings.

The less public manifestations of my father's inner life—those only a few of us were privy to—included his commitment to providing employment for those in the most need, his behind-the-scenes generosity to various causes, and his unmitigated devotion to my mother. A handful of long-time employees of Hoerr Nursery, I came to realize over the years, were not kept on the payroll because they were top performers—not even close in many cases. Rather, my dad saw an opportunity to provide gainful employment, meaningful work, to those who perhaps needed it the most. It was really these less public expressions of Dad's faith that made it palpable and real, something much more tangible than just an ideology or doctrine.

While Dad's faith was certainly authentic, I had a difficult time separating my view of him as one who expected us to work hard and do everything with excellence, with consequences for failing to do so, from my view of God. That's where my mother came in. In many ways, she was the embodiment of love and acceptance that everyone so intensely desires. Regardless of my up and down test scores, Little League misadventures, D's in conduct, and assorted other youthful shenanigans, she loved me as nearly unconditionally as anyone can. She seemed the authentic, tangible representation of the feminine side of the Godhead—soft, gentle, embracing, warm, present. She was the grace of God in the flesh. I recall a special memory from second grade, spring of 1967:

"Hey, Mom!" I said as I burst into the slate-floored utility room at the back of the house.

"Timmy! I missed you today! It's getting late in the day, you know."

"Look at these papers from today. Miss Owen said I did really well on the math test!"

"Well, I was getting a bit worried about you. You're normally home at three-thirty. It's nearly four-thirty. I was about ready to come looking for you, little man." Her look of concern prompted an explanation.

"Oh, I stayed afterwards to wash the blackboards, pick up trash, and empty the pencil sharpener for Miss Owen. She is really nice. I might marry her someday," I said.

Mom smiled and gave me a big hug. "Aha, so that's it," she said. "I figured it might be something like that. She is pretty special. You did have me worried, though. I'm so glad you're okay."

Delivering the news of my day to my mom was always a highlight for me. Those after-school interactions—my daily dose of hugs and motherly doting—gave meaning to my day and reassured me that that the world was in order, I was loved and significant, and that whatever problems I faced, I would somehow solve.

So between my parents' lives and their embodiment of godly characteristics (that were distinctly different from one another), I can always remember having a deep, deep desire to follow God. It seemed to work well for them, though not perfectly, of course. Why wouldn't I want something that worked, and that seemed to make good sense of life's conundrums and difficulties? I would describe it now as a very real yearning to get in sync with God's bigger plan and purpose for the earth.

The first memory of this phenomenon was when I was perhaps 5 or 6 years old, but the clearest such early memory was an incident in fifth grade (1971) where I felt the overwhelming, powerful, all-encompassing presence of God on the patio outside the family room.

The light summer breezes were rustling the leaves of the large red oak that overhung the edge of our brick patio. The hornbeam trees, five of them arranged sentry-like in an arc on the perimeter, provided protection from the elements and shade to boot. The afternoon sun was filtering through the oak and hornbeams now, casting fanciful shadows. I sat in the swing thinking that this must surely be what heaven would be like. So beautiful, so peaceful, yet very real, touchable, available to be experienced with my human senses.

As I sat there in that peace, I heard a voice say, "I am with you. I am calling you. I love you. I want you to know me."

A warm sensation came over me. The voice wasn't audible; I heard it in my head and felt it in my heart. But it was as real as real can be. Someone was speaking to me, reaching out to me, challenging me.

Now, this experience was something quite apart from what I knew of God from the Apostolic Christian Church Sunday School. There, complete with flannel board cut-outs of Bible characters, I had heard and seen stories about Daniel in the Lion's Den, David and Goliath, and Joshua leading the Israelites to conquer Canaan. I'd seen Jesus, the most glorious cardboard cutout figure of all, with a lamb draped around his shoulders, kneeling to embrace a circle of children. I had understood that the whole point of all these stories was believing in a certain way so that I could inherit "eternal life," a disembodied existence of bliss in the by-and-by. And God, the ruler of this eternal realm, was the man on the flannel board—well, sort of. God and Jesus were basically the same person, merged into one in my mind. Not terribly tangible, and certainly not personal.

Yet as I sat on my patio that afternoon, I knew I had just encountered Jesus. In a very personal way. He had enveloped me, loved me and issued a call to enter into a relationship with him. That much was unmistakable. Through it all, I was provoked to ask the questions "Who is Jesus?" and "How do I respond to him?"

In this immersion into an almost-alternate-reality, I encountered amazing peace and extreme joy to an extent I had never felt. I did not understand it at the time, but I would now characterize the experience as a blanketing by the Spirit presence of God. Indeed, this was the first time I remember experiencing a tangible "power encounter" with the person of God. It was real, almost tangible, and yet mystical. While I previously had a sense of who God was, primarily through observance of my parents' actions, I had never experienced a direct connection to Jesus.

So, what to do with this very cool experience? Tell someone? My mother, perhaps? Yes, that made sense. Minutes later, I thought better of it. This type of thing didn't categorize easily and seemed completely off the grid with what I knew to be normal and acceptable. I decided to stay quiet, perhaps as constrained by an inability to articulate what had happened as I was fearful of what others might think. I knew something profound had happened, but I kept it to myself.

In the ensuing years, I carried on regular dialogue with Jesus in my attempt to answer the question of just who he was and what was the nature of my relationship with him. Or maybe I should call it a monologue, because in the most child-like way, it consisted mostly of my requests—to do well on tests, to become more athletic, for sick relatives to get better, that sort of thing. The Church had told me that until I reached the vaguely defined "age of accountability," I couldn't really be in any kind of relationship with God, so all of this was on the hush-hush. Nevertheless, the one-sided conversations continued. And while I certainly enjoyed a range of childhood adventures, nothing came close to what I'd experienced that summer day on the patio until much later in my teen years. Today, I'm still asking the question—and finding a multiplicity of answers—that is in some sense at the core of all other questions I've asked in my life: "Who is Jesus?"

3. Seeds of Entrepreneurship

Peoria, Illinois
June 1975

IT WAS LATE AFTERNOON ON A SATURDAY IN EARLY JUNE. I was 13 at the time. Hoerr's Garden Center had been particularly busy that day. We were running a sale on shade trees, now that the prime spring season was winding to a close. We had decided to offer an incentive to customers to extend the spring planting season into summer by reducing prices by 30%, and boy did they respond. All day long, I had traipsed through rows of balled and burlapped ashes, maples, birches, and sweet gums, pointing out the ones I thought were particularly nice-looking to the customer I was serving. Once selected, I used a forklift to load the tree into the customer's vehicle or place it in the holding area for delivery. I would then meet them at the cash register to finalize the sale—only to turn around and repeat the cycle with the next customer awaiting service. Catching only a couple of brief breaks throughout the day, I was exhausted, hungry, and ready to go home. But not before I tackled my final and favorite work task.

I clutched my lower back as little rills of pain spiked through my body, walking past the disheveled boxes of grass seed and bottles of Diazinon. Customers sure can create a mess of things! I chuckled to myself, figuring I'd have something to do first thing on Monday morning. The task list at the garden center never did get completed—it simply rolled from one workday to the next, with fresh new jobs waiting every morning. (Sort of like the Lord's compassions… but not quite.)

Entering the accounting office, just off the main sales floor at the garden center, Betty McCumber was already working on closing out the day's sales report.

"I'm all ready for you, Timmy."

"Mrs. McCumber, its Tim, not Timmy. I'm thirteen now."

"Oh, right. Sorry about that. Old habits are hard to break. My, you look beat. Busy day, huh?"

"For sure. Customers really liked the shade tree sale prices. I think I took a ten-minute lunch break, at best."

"Well, if you'd like to hit the road early, I understand. I can handle the closing process alone tonight," Betty said.

"Oh, no. I wouldn't want to miss my favorite part of the day."

"Of course! Mine too!" Betty laughed.

While Betty tallied sales figures from each register, I took the cash bags, stuffed with receipts, charge card slips, and of course, fat stacks of green bills. Counting out the money and laying it in neat piles of ones, fives, tens, and twenties gave me a thrill. The authentic feel of U.S. currency, the familiar smell of well-worn bills, the little stacks each in their place, all combined to bring a certain sense of satisfaction and completeness, of order and tidiness, to an otherwise complicated world. As a bonus, the task of tying out the cash and charge slip totals to the register tallies, though sometimes challenging, conveyed the idea that some problems in life are indeed solvable. Part A can be reconciled and brought into harmony with Part B.

"Looks like everything is tying out just fine tonight." I said, with an exaggerated exhale, magnifying my sense of accomplishment.

"Oh, good, Timmy, er… Tim. That's great."

"Here are the tie-out sheets, Mrs. McCumber. I'll see you on Monday morning. Enjoy your Sunday off!"

I gathered up my lunch pail, iced tea jug and pocketknife, smiling to myself. At the end of a busy day at Hoerr's Nursery Garden Center, some things actually made sense. We offered beautiful living things to the public, they purchased them in anticipation of making their small corner of the world more delightful, and cash was exchanged. The cash was sorted into neat piles and a tally was prepared for the bank. The tally tied out to what the register said we sold. Then we could pay our employees, buy more plants, perhaps purchase a new piece of equipment, and have a profit left over. This at its most fundamental level is American capitalism in general and entrepreneurship in particular. And though not all problems in business are as easily resolved as tying out the fat stacks of green dollar bills to the register records, business done well can indeed cooperate with and contribute to God's bigger scheme of "setting things right in the world" (a phrase mentioned dozens of times throughout scripture). How so?

In Genesis 1:26-28, we find the following passage:

> God spoke: "Let us make human beings in our image, make them reflecting our nature so they can be responsible for the fish in the sea, the birds in the air, the cattle, and, yes, Earth itself, and every animal that moves on the face of Earth." God created human beings; he created them godlike, reflecting God's nature. He created them male and female. God blessed them: "Prosper! Reproduce! Fill Earth! Take charge! Be responsible for fish in the sea and birds in the air, for every living thing that moves on the face of Earth." (*The Message*)

There are a number of fascinating elements to this particular scripture. We are created in the very image of God—so we, too, are creators. We are created in relationship with each other. And, we are created with a purpose—to prosper, reproduce, fill the earth, and take charge. There are, of course, infinite ways in which "taking charge" can be lived out—as a schoolteacher impacting young lives, as a songwriter creating inspiring music, as a scientist making new discoveries, and certainly as an entrepreneur offering a product or service that meets a specific need and contributes to the common good. Entrepreneurs, in particular, have the opportunity to create solutions that solve practical problems while building an organization that brings together the talents of many toward a singular goal. And if this is done well, one more piece of the world's brokenness becomes fixed or set right.

What I didn't fully appreciate at the tender age of 13, however, were the difficult challenges and significant risks being taken by my father and his co-owner brothers in building their business. There were the complexities of finance, operations, strategy, and competitive positioning, navigated by long hours of behind-the-scenes work in order to produce sustained success. I didn't understand the nuances and challenges of bringing together people, capital, resources, and opportunity to meet the needs of customers and grow a business.

But over time, I would learn. Beginning the summer after fifth grade and continuing through the end of my college education, I worked in nearly every area of the business. Landscaping: check. Sod farm: check. Tree nursery: check. Landscape architecture and design: check. Garden center. Well, you get the idea. From the most mundane of assignments—sweeping the fertilizer warehouse, pulling weeds, watering impatiens and geraniums, to the more fulfilling jobs, such as designing a landscape plan to solve a unique set of problems, installing a retaining wall constructed of boulders, and educating customers on which plants did best in certain conditions—I was baptized into the fundamentals of entrepreneurship.

It was challenging and tiring work. By the time mid-August arrived, I was counting the days until the start of school—which meant I was only conscripted to work on weekends. Sweet relief. The lessons learned were compelling nonetheless. And though I did not realize it at the time, entrepreneurship was my destiny. Not only to be an entrepreneur, with all of its thrills, dips, crescendos, and moments of sheer terror, but to eventually be a catalyst for those desiring to be entrepreneurs. To encourage young men and women to step out of the place of comfort and security (real or imagined)—to risk it—and take the entrepreneurial plunge! I would not realize the beckoning of this entrepreneurial destiny until years later, but the little rootlets that sprouted in my teenage days would later become a bulwark, a fully-developed root system underlying my fundamental understanding and practice of business to this day.

4. Pearls in the Poop

Peoria, Illinois
July 1976

ONE AFTERNOON WHEN I WAS FOURTEEN, after I had finished watering a row of maple trees, I walked into the garden center to check in with my dad about my next task. I couldn't find him, but I did see a burly man with gray sideburns and thick glasses approach me. He eyed me suspiciously, as if he wasn't sure if I could be trusted with his request.

"Do you work here?" he asked, rather gruffly.

"I do. How can I help you?"

"I need some plants delivered to my house. I was in to pick them out yesterday. I think someone put my name on the ones I picked. Here's a list of the plants."

He handed me his list. I noticed he was still eyeing me suspiciously.

"We can definitely deliver them," I said, trying to sound helpful, authoritative, and friendly all at once. "Do you want to step over to the register?"

He nodded, and as I walked over to the register, he followed me. I rang up the sale. "With tax and the delivery charge, that'll be $248.65."

The man furrowed his brow. "Delivery charge! What are you talking about?"

"Well, sir, we charge $10 for deliveries."

"Surely you don't charge for an order of this size," the man said, his cheeks reddening.

"We do, sir," I said, as I refrained from telling him we regularly got orders much larger than his. "It's our policy."

"That's absurd. I'm not paying any delivery charge," the man said. He apparently thought he was royalty and was above such petty charges.

"I'm sorry, sir, but you'll have to, to get your plants delivered."

The man glared long and hard at me, expecting me to back down, I'm sure. But I stuck to my guns. I knew I'd have my dad to answer to if I deducted the delivery charge. It wasn't even an option. Besides, this guy was not endearing himself to me any too quickly. But I kept as pleasant a demeanor as I could.

"I want to talk to your manager," the man said in a low growl that I knew was meant to be threatening.

"Sir, my manager is my dad, and he owns the nursery, and he sets the policy, and he doesn't waver from it," I said as cheerfully as possible.

"You're saying you won't waive that delivery charge?"

"Yes, sir. Sorry, sir."

He scowled at me. I thought he was about to burst a vein in his neck. "A fine businessman you'll make!" he said. "Have you ever heard the saying that the customer is always right? Has that ever passed your ears?"

"Yes sir, but I really can't change the store policy."

He shook his head, as if he had never run into anyone so impudent and dull-witted in his entire life.

"Fine, then!" he said. "Cancel my order. I don't want any of it! I'll take my business elsewhere!"

With that, he stormed off, and as I watched him go, I felt sick to my stomach. I noticed I was visibly shaking, and I felt my face was flushed. My brother Ben, who was walking by, stopped when he saw me.

"Hey, you okay?" he asked.

"Yeah, I guess." I told him what had happened. He grinned and slapped my shoulder.

"Chalk it up to a learning experience," he said. "And you know what? The customer was right. He said he wasn't going to pay any delivery charge... and he didn't!"

I nodded, and was thankful he was trying to make me feel better, but for the rest of the afternoon, as I applied pesticide to various rows of trees, I went over and over my exchange with that "gentleman." I kept looking for clues as to what I'd done wrong, but I didn't find any. Yet that man was so mad at me that I thought he was going to spit at me. I'd never encountered a customer who'd objected so vehemently to such a trivial fee.

There had to be some pearls in the poop, however. As Ben said, it was a learning experience. So what had I learned?

I finally settled on four pearls:

- One, operating a successful business involves dealing with a wide range of customers—not all of whom are considerate or rational.
- Two, the core of a successful business is serving people. A team of employees that exudes an authentic attitude of helping others, even tough customers, is often the "X factor" in making an enterprise successful in the long run.
- Three, business is not easy. (Maybe that's why they call it "work.") Any time you have humans interacting, you have the chance for difficulties, disagreements, and challenges.
- Lastly, I was determined to prove this guy wrong. I would become a learner, always seeking out new knowledge to improve my business skills. I would commit to being excellent in my work. And, I would, in fact, become a "fine businessman"—whatever that meant and whatever it took. Unknowingly to him, this unhappy customer had thrown down the gauntlet and challenged me—and my competitive nature was intent on rising to the challenge!

5. A God Encounter at Turkey Run

Turkey Run State Park, Indiana
July 1977

I WAS SITTING DOWN, TAKING MY PLACE AT OUR YOUTH GROUP CHOIR PRACTICE on a Wednesday evening, when I noticed Max walking toward me. He plopped himself in the seat next to me, there in the basement of the Apostolic Christian Church.

"Hey, Tim, you going on the youth group canoe trip to Turkey Run State Park?" he asked. Max was one of my good buddies from youth group and a distant cousin to boot.

"Of course! Wouldn't miss it, man. I hear Sugar Creek is really high this year—should make for some fun in the sun!"

Our high school youth group embarked on periodic adventures, most of them relatively close to home. The trip to Turkey Run State Park was special, though. About three hours east of Peoria via Interstate 74, Turkey Run is a spectacular combination of canyons, challenging hiking trails, and the meandering Sugar Creek. It really is a natural gem, enhanced by great facilities and amenities. A couple of canoe outfitters provide a range of trips for groups of all sizes and varying degrees of skill. Our group was slated for the moderate, ten-mile trip that Saturday in June, 1977. Coolers were packed with sandwiches and sodas. Hats, sunglasses, and tanning lotion were a must. As the tour bus sped past what would become my future home, Champaign, I eagerly anticipated the adventures of the day. The sun was shining brightly. Temps in the high 70s were forecast. What could be better than canoeing down Sugar Creek with your buddies, not to mention having some fine-looking young ladies to tease?

"You wanna canoe together, Jeff?" I asked my cousin, sitting across the aisle from me. Pairing off was part of the drill, with some folks saying "yes" and then "no" two or three times until settling in on the right canoeing partner.

"Sure. Why not," Jeff said.

Jeff was a special relative and friend. Born four days apart (our moms shared the same hospital room that December of 1961!), we grew up across the street from each other and generally did most of life in tandem.

"We need to make sure and do our best to dump Linda and Holly in the drink," I smirked. We were targeting these two, of course, because they were among the cutest in the youth group.

"Oh, definitely. That's half the fun!" Jeff laughed.

The bus crossed the Indiana state line and about 15 miles later turned south on U.S. Route 41. Shortly, the topography changed dramatically. Over the next 20 miles, we wound through rolling hills and densely forested areas—much different than the flat corn and soybean fields we had seen most of the way along our interstate journey. Arriving at the outfitter parking area, our group of about 60 disembarked the bus, gathered our coolers and gear, and loaded into the outfitter's school bus for the ten-mile trip upstream. There, we were assigned canoes, paddles, and life vests (not used by most of the boys, mind you).

At about 10 a.m., Jeff and I loaded our canoe and shoved off. The chaotic launching of dozens of canoes, with people laughing and splashing one another, some canoes tipping over immediately, coolers and gear spilling into the creek, soon gave way to a more serene experience as canoes began to separate from one another. Jeff and I proceeded at a pretty leisurely pace, talking about a variety of topics with little depth or substance—our mutual fondness for the Chicago Cubs, our shared experience of playing in the Richwoods High School marching band (both baritone players), and working together at Hoerr Nursery.

About noon, as we passed through a deep canyon rimmed with oaks, maples, and birches, with the sun peaked overhead, I felt it again. That same warm and surrounding sensation I'd experienced so many years prior on the patio. The powerful presence of God's Spirit cloaked me, washed over me. I was at a loss for words.

"What's up?" Jeff asked, noticing that our rambling conversation had turned quiet.

"I don't know. It's weird. I can't explain it."

"What do you mean? What's weird?"

"Do you feel something different?" I asked.

"Not particularly. I mean, this is a cool place and everything. Is that what you mean?"

I shook my head. "It's more than that," I said. "I don't know how to say it, exactly. Other than to say God is here."

And with that, the conversation pretty much went completely quiet for the next half hour or so. Jeff wasn't sure what to do with it—and neither was I. But there it was again. A sense of God's presence, but more specifically, a calling. God visiting me, but not as an end in itself. There was purpose and promise here.

And there, floating down that creek, I heard his voice again: "Something big is going on. I want you to cooperate with it. Yield to me in the process. I love you. I am calling you." Again, it wasn't audible, but that wonderful and confusing message was impressed in my heart. I had no doubt that God was telling me this. I just didn't know what it meant or what to do with it.

Something big is going on? I need to cooperate with it? What did that mean? I didn't understand it, but I sensed that the next step was to make a more intentional commitment to respond to the Caller. As a teenager, I was just beginning to understand the ramifications of making wise choices, the inherent power of goal setting, and the consequences of my day-to-day actions. And so, as we dodged a large tree that had fallen into Sugar Creek, I knew my destiny was to press into the Person issuing the call, to align myself with this "bigger plan"—and to have something more than just a one-sided conversation with the Creator of the universe!

The next two years of high school and the years continuing into college were ones of phenomenal life change as I plunged into a deepening relationship with God. I wanted to fully understand this bigger story, to make sense of it all. And I wanted to experience all that God had for me, in the most authentic way possible. I read the scriptures. I read books. I sought out friends who were on a similar journey. I prayed and listened for answers. For most of that time, I got only glimpses of the bigger story. I knew there was something more, and that frustrated me. In the middle of it all, however, I did feel at home, at peace.

As Jeff and I drifted down that creek, with only the birds and our oars dipping into the water breaking the silence, I pondered what was happening. Perhaps this is only the starting point, I thought. A point where I find a place of peace and identity in the One who created me.

And perhaps from that foundation, I deduced, there was a profound journey ahead.

6. Real Freedom

Peoria, Illinois
August 1977

ON A SUMMER MORNING WHEN I WAS 15, I'd gone to work anticipating working in the sales department for the day. Dean Ramseyer, Garden Center manager, had told me the evening before that he really appreciated the way I was interacting with customers and he wanted me to spend more time in the sales and customer service function. I'd been working in the business since fifth grade—and I had covered the gamut of tasks over the years. Working in sales was probably my favorite assignment, but it seemed I was always being pulled off for less glamorous duties! More time in sales was music to my ears—a rescue, of sorts, from toiling in obscurity with what I perceived as "gofer" tasks of watering, weed pulling, shelf stocking, and mowing.

I'd gone home the evening before with lightness in my feet. I'd arrived!

"Hey, Mom, guess what?" I said as I walked into the kitchen, where she was checking on her meatloaf in the oven.

"Hmmm. Let me guess," she said as she closed the oven door. "You lost the thermos from your lunch bucket again?"

"Aw, come on Mom, give me a break. I'm being promoted. Well, kind of!"

"Promoted, eh? That sounds pretty neat. What's Dad got for you?"

"Well, it's not Dad, its Dean. And he's got me on the sales department schedule all day tomorrow!"

"Wow, Tim, that's just super. I know you enjoy working in sales just about as much as anything at the garden center. Good for you!"

Dinner never tasted better. Of course, Mom's meatloaf was one of my favorites. Sleep was sweeter, too. I woke early, raring to go.

Crossing the parking lot at the nursery, I saw my Dad, who yelled out, "Hey, Tim, come over here."

As I walked over to him, I called out, "What is it, Dad?"

"Well, I was in the fertilizer warehouse this morning, and it's a complete mess. Busted bags. Collections of junk piled here and there. Pallets out of order. It's a wonder anyone can find a thing in there. I doubt we've cleaned that out any time in the last six months."

"Hmm. Sounds like the place needs an overhaul, Dad—probably an all-day chore. Maybe Bob or Jeff could get on that. I'm working sales today."

"Well, Tim, I was thinking you'd be the man for the job. What do you say you grab Jeff to help, and you two get on that first thing this morning? There's a good crew working in sales today, and I'd really like that warehouse sparkling as soon as possible."

My facial expression and body language must have belied my utter disappointment.

"Aw, come on now, Tim. Buck up. You gotta take the bitter with the sweet!" Dad said.

The day of my imminent promotion to a job with real meaning and I was being assigned the gofer job of all gofer jobs: cleaning and sorting the fertilizer warehouse. Unbelievable.

"Dad, really? Dean Ramseyer asked me to work sales. I was…"

"You'll be just fine, Tim. Sales can wait another day," Dad interrupted.

So much for empathy.

I proceeded to hunt down my cousin Jeff and we spent the day sorting, sweeping, cleaning, throwing out, moving around, and organizing over 100 pallets of fertilizer, pesticides, and wood chips. We both stood back with a sense of accomplishment, disappointed though I was at not getting a crack at sales that day.

My dad came by at 4 p.m. to inspect the work we'd done, and I was convinced he would be impressed. After all, we'd busted tail to make the best of what started as a pretty ugly situation.

"Well, you guys did pretty good, and it's definitely an improvement… but I want to show you a few things," he said after he surveyed our work.

Dad proceeded to point out three or four things we could have done better: consolidating like fertilizers in the same section; stacking the unused pallets by type, not just putting all of them in one mixed pile; and fixing some of the signage that identified where things were supposed to go. Hmmm. Those things hadn't been on his list of instructions—and you might say they required either a little mind reading or at least some thinking outside the box for a 16-year-old. I was now doubly disappointed—not only had I missed out on my day in sales, but I hadn't measured up to being a very good gofer either.

For some strange reason, the memory of that day lingers with me, powerfully, many decades later. In years of working at the nursery, I can remember only a handful of truly significant moments like this. It had a two-edged quality to it, as I now recall.

There were some pearls of wisdom to be sure.
- Don't count those chickens until they are hatched.
- Ask for more specificity in the job deliverables, perhaps.
- Learn to think outside the box and go above the immediate thing being asked.

All valuable lessons that have served me well, pushing me to perform at the highest level possible.

But there was something else that happened that day. I got the sense that my Dad was not perfectly pleased with me, and in fact, would never be so, no matter the effort exerted or the end deliverable accomplished. There would always be three or four things I could improve upon. That day, the vague notion that I had wrestled with as a child and into teenage days became more stark and tangible, whether or not precisely accurate. That perceived truth was hard to swallow. But it is a reality that I now know many people have been forced to embrace: We will let people down. And people will let us down, in turn.

But I also made a dangerous leap in logic that day from the understanding that I wasn't "good enough" for my Dad, to believing that I was not good enough for God. That he, too, expected me to do just a bit better. Even in situations where I thought I'd done a pretty good job. Unfortunately, this skewed view of God—that I somehow needed to perform in order to gain his approval—provided a dysfunctional and distorted foundation well into my 30s and early 40s. As long as I could perform the task at hand—and keep doing better—I felt okay about myself because I figured God was smiling and nodding. Only in the last decade or so have I come to realize that I am loved and accepted unconditionally by the Father regardless of my behavior or performance.

This realization came through a series of life circumstances, most notably a very rough period of back-to-back-to-back failures in the late 1990s after I left the position of partner in a public accounting firm and took the risk of becoming an entrepreneur (I share more extensively about this in Part 2 of the book). In a certain way, the failures took me to the end of myself, destroying my most deeply held beliefs about my personal strengths and competencies and nearly derailing me permanently from the path of entrepreneurship. Up to that time, I had always been able to perform, to succeed, to move forward to the next challenge. And my ability to perform at a very high level had given me an aggrandized sense of self-worth. But during those two years, I failed at nearly everything I tried.

Still, in the middle of what I would deem the most difficult and disheartening time in my life, I felt loved by God and accepted by him in the most profound way. He showed me that my personal performance as an entrepreneur had nothing to do with my standing as his son. And once I grasped that truth, it emboldened me to live, work, and relate to others from a place of ultimate security and significance. Because I knew that I was loved and accepted as a son, regardless of my performance, I became truly free.

7. Set Apart

Peoria, Illinois
September 1977

I WAITED UNTIL ALL THE STUDENTS HAD LEFT THE BAND ROOM and drew a deep breath as I approached Mr. Christiansen, the director of the concert band at Richwoods High School.

"Uh, Mr. Christiansen, do you have a minute?" I said, averting my eyes as he looked at me.

"Sure, Tim. What can I do for you?"

"Well, uh, I, uh… I have to quit band."

He stared at me blankly for a moment, as if he hadn't heard correctly. "You have to what?"

"I can't play anymore," I said, feeling rather helpless and puny and hoping against hope he wouldn't ask why.

"Tim. You are first chair baritone. We have a football game Friday night. I need you to march on Friday night," he said.

"I know, but I can't play in the band anymore," I said, as if that would clear everything up.

"What in the world are you talking about?" he said, furrowing his brow and looking at me as if I were speaking Chinese.

I sucked in another breath and took the plunge. "Well, it's... uh, my church... well, it's against my religious principles to play in the band."

"Your religious what?"

I didn't expect him to understand. And he was living up to my expectations.

"My church doesn't think that I should be playing in the band. I mean, that anyone should. Not just me," I said. As if all bands should be abolished. That hadn't come out well. Not that any of it had.

"What does a religious principle have to do with playing the baritone?" Mr. Christiansen said, his face reddening and a neck vein beginning to bulge. I wondered if it would pop before I managed to drag myself out of the room.

"Uh, I don't know..." I said. I felt sweat trickling down my back. I felt a sudden longing to get to my geometry class. Or to go get a root canal. Anything other than this.

"And what I am supposed to do about Friday night? And the next Friday night? And about the whole football season, and the fall concert for that matter?" he asked in rapid-fire staccato. His eyes were aflame, piercing me. Deeply.

I shuddered and looked at the top of my sneakers. He had a good point. An excellent one, in fact. I didn't think he'd understand that playing in the band equated, for my church, to playing with fire—that it was a "worldly" activity that set me on a slippery slope of sinfulness. I doubted he saw music in that light. So, in my less-than-infinite wisdom, I withheld that damning information from him.

"Well, sir, I don't know what to say. I, well, I..."

"Well, what? You don't seem to have thought this through very well, Mr. Hoerr. Why don't you think about it some more. Put yourself in my shoes. And come back tomorrow to discuss it."

"Mr. Christiansen, my decision... I've made up my mind. I don't think that thinking about it for another day is going to help much. As a new Christian, I have to act consistently with my beliefs, and I just cannot stay a part of the band." I felt as if I had turned into a fish, and I was flopping on a riverbank, trying to find the water. And getting weaker and more desperate by the second.

"It doesn't seem very Christian to me!" He got up, waved me out the door with an exaggerated gesture, and slammed it behind me.

And so began my rather painful withdrawal from the world, one of the chief dictates of the church in which I'd grown up, the church I was now in the process of officially joining. Following my overwhelming experience with God's Spirit on Sugar Creek in Turkey Run State Park, I did what all new believers in this particular faith tradition did. I systematically began to redefine my relationships, my activities, my entire lifestyle, to align with God's, er, the church's mandates, its protocol for becoming a "real Christian." And, according to the church, to be Christian meant most importantly to be holy, separate from the world—hence, I was to "come out from among them." And them meant pretty much anyone and anything that had previously meant something to me but which no longer met the definition of holy, sanctified, separate. In other words, anyone or anything that was not connected to my church.

My prized first chair baritone seat in the concert band was the first to go. My affiliation with the debate team was next. Participating in theater? Another ungodly association; it had to go. But most painful of all was the emotionally charged act of changing lunch tables, leaving the group that had been my best friends from 7th grade on and choosing the group of fellow separatists (we didn't call ourselves that, mind you!). It was painful. It was labored. It was unnatural. And, that, I was told, made it all the more authentic.

"Tim, we're over here, man." Steve Enda called out, waving me over as I walked past my friends' table.

"Uh, yeah, sorry Steve. I'm, uh, going to eat with these guys today," I muttered as I walked slowly past.

"What?"

"I said I'm going to eat lunch over here today, Steve." My face flushed, my body temperature rose. Little beads of perspiration formed on the back of my neck.

"You're going to what?" Steve asked, now at a decibel level that half of the cafeteria could probably hear.

"I'm sorry, man. Can we talk about this later?"

"Your choice, man. Weird." Steve, bewildered, shook his head.

My emotions were awhirl, my mind was racing, my body was now saturated in sweat. Was withdrawing from the world supposed to be this hard? I sat next to Larry, my friend from church, unable to summon an appetite. I sat for 20 minutes in silence, alone with my confusion and angst.

The separatism journey continued for the next two years, my junior and senior years of high school. Not only was participating in such worldly activities as concert band and theater forbidden, but attending was as well. I became increasingly frustrated at the colorless existence I was leading. It was hard enough being a late-blooming teenager struggling to find my identity and place in the world. This wasn't making it any easier.

"Hey, Tim, we're having a party this weekend at Steve's house. You want to come?" Matt Yeomans yelled across the hallway one afternoon about a year after I had begun my withdrawal process.

Okay, had Matt not gotten the memo yet? Had he not noticed how holy, or at least separate, I had become in the last year?

"Oh, hey, thanks for the invitation, Matt. I'm pretty busy this weekend."

"You're always busy. When are you going to get over this church thing and be real again?"

So he had gotten the memo. He was just expecting me to snap out of it, like a man coming out of a coma.

"Matt, it's like this. I'm not getting over the church thing. It's who I am now. I know it doesn't make much sense to you," I replied, trying hard to believe what I was saying. Truth was, it didn't make much sense to me, either.

"You got that right. I liked the old version of you much better, man. I mean, you were pretty cool and all—but now, I mean, if this is what Christianity is all about, then I don't want any part of it." Matt walked away, shaking his head. I'd seen a lot of that head-shaking over the last couple of years.

I stared blankly down the hallway as Matt walked past the colorful and zany homecoming posters. Senior year. We were the "kings of the hill" here at Richwoods High. This was supposed to be the pinnacle, the top of the heap. But I had become completely detached, in what had become a systematic dismantling of relationships and things that had previously made sense. Things that had given me great pleasure and meaning. Music. Theater. Sports. Old friends. I'd said no to them all. But my ill-constructed and outwardly-influenced quest for asceticism seemed to be cracking, failing, leaving me dry and thirsty.

I felt a deep pain in my chest as Matt disappeared around the corner at the end of the hallway, making his way toward Mrs. Sathoff's calculus class. Is this what it meant to be the "light of the world"? Was my "testimony" really working? Yes, there were glimpses of God in the middle of it all, yet nothing quite like I'd experienced on my patio that summer afternoon or on the canoe trip that seemed to start it all. Not only was I not happy, but others seemed to care little for what I had. In fact, most wanted no part of it at all—like it was a disease or something.

I was driving away the handful of people who were trying to give me another chance at friendship, despite my best efforts to cut them off. Maybe, just maybe, there was a different approach to this whole thing. Maybe I could find a way to serve and experience God without cutting off the "world." My brain hurt thinking about it. But the deeper pain in my soul told me I needed to press in more deeply, to find a way that worked. Because the path I'd been following wasn't working. My old friends didn't like the new me, and I can't say that I blamed them.

8. It Added Up

Peoria, Illinois
August 1978

MY DAD TURNED HIS PICKUP FROM SHADETREE DRIVE ONTO ROUTE 91. We were on our way home from a warm summer Saturday's work at the nursery. My T-shirt was damp with sweat, but the air conditioner was starting to cool me off. As he headed south on 91, he said, "So have you figured out your major yet?"

I would be headed to college in about a year, but I still wasn't sure what I was going to do. "Not really," I said. And not really wanting to talk about it, either.

"I think you should boil down your choices as best you can." My dad said this confidently, as if he knew my career direction as well as he knew our route home.

I was tired and I was primarily concerned with getting home and drinking about a gallon of sweetened ice tea. That was the choice I was most concerned with at the moment. But I knew he wouldn't let the conversation wane, so I tried to give a perfunctory answer in hopes it would cut him off.

"Well, it's sort of tough to say. There are a lot of good choices out there. I'm sure I'll figure it out once I get there," I said, sneaking a glance at him to see if this would satisfy him.

It wouldn't. I could see him deep in thought as he turned east onto 150. I braced myself for further discussion on a topic that I frankly didn't care about at the moment. I would have told my dad to chill, but he was not the sort of dad you told this to.

"So tell me your interests," he said.

"You mean other than drinking some cold ice tea and getting cleaned up?"

He gave me a look that needed no words.

"Okay," I said. "I don't know." I prodded my brain for a moment. It didn't like being prodded about this stuff in the middle of summer. "Chemistry, pre-med, business, literature, law. I'm sort of interested in all of them. How am I supposed to know what I want to do with my life?"

My father gave me a brief smile. I could see he was happy I was playing his game.

"You're not really supposed to know, though that's what society tells you," he said. "Look, if you're struggling a bit, here's my advice. Narrow it down to three options." He said this last bit with a certain zest. It almost sounded rehearsed. As if he had already narrowed down my best three options and couldn't wait to share them with me.

"And which three would those be, Dad?" I said in a rather cavalier tone, which my father chose to ignore.

"Number one: landscape architecture," he said. "That's what your brother is studying at the University of Illinois, and it seems to be working out well for him."

"Hmmm," I said, training my eyes on the line of traffic moving toward us. "Not my bag. I've worked enough on landscape crews over the last few years, and I'm pretty sure that's not going to cut it for me. What's number two?"

"Horticulture. It's awfully useful, particularly if you're looking at joining the family business someday."

I couldn't help but laugh. "Number two sounds quite a bit like number one to me, Dad. I like plants and everything, but I can't see myself propagating euonymus alatus and quercus alba for the next thirty years. Nice as a hobby, but as a career, pretty uninteresting stuff."

We seemed to be in a verbal jousting match of sorts, and Dad was clearly enjoying himself.

"I beg your pardon, young man. Horticulture can be quite amazing and in fact, quite interesting. It's not just propagation. It's species cross-breeding. It's understanding which plants work best in certain landscape conditions. It's seeing how trees and shrubs fit into the larger ecological environment. Why, if you think about it…"

"Whoa, whoa. I get your point," I said, holding up a hand to stop his horticultural rhapsody. "Fascinating stuff, Dad. Not for me. What's the third option on your list?"

He looked over at me, lifting an eyebrow in appraisal before playing his trump card.

"Accounting," he said. "It's the language of business, and we certainly need folks who understand business here at the nursery."

Dad had saved accounting for last, and for good reason. He knew me better than I realized. The other two options had been setups, I surmised. Mentioned merely to contrast with Dad's hand-selected choice for me. And, quite effective, I might add! This interchange, I've come to understand, is known as scripting others. It's something most of us do, to some extent—and particularly with our kids. We want the best for them. We think we know what's best. So, we write the script and present it to them and in some cases, sell it to them. Hard.

And the hard sell was working pretty effectively on me that evening. While I'd had a sense of calling for many years, it hadn't solidified into anything more specific as I approached a major point of decision for many teens—the choice of a college major. But Dad had picked up on an emerging theme in my life—the desire to be a businessman, an entrepreneur—and he had noticed that I possessed some good, raw skills that might lend themselves to being pretty effective in business down the road.

"Accounting, huh?" As I mulled over the thought, I began to feel excited and energized.

"Sure. Think about it, Tim. You've always been intrigued with business, with customer relationships that become transactions, and with the larger systems at work behind the scenes. Accounting will help you develop that interest in a meaningful way, perhaps more than other business disciplines."

This was starting to make sense to me. More importantly, an unlocked energy was being released and my mind began to dance with the possibilities. I did like numbers. I loved the experience of working with the public, the nuances of relating to and serving customers. And, those stacks of green dollar bills at the end of a busy day at the garden center had a magical appeal. Gaining a better understanding of how all of the pieces fit together—how products, services, systems, marketing, sales, service, and the like could come together in a functional way to produce those wonderful little stacks of cash—now, that would be fascinating! Accounting it was.

9. A Redbird Spreads His Wings

Normal, Illinois
August 1979

WALKING UP THE STEPS FROM MY BASEMENT APARTMENT on Dillon Drive in Normal, Illinois, my mom said, "Just a couple more loads and we'll be finished." Moving past her as I carried two boxes of clothes and shoes, I felt a lump in my throat as I saw the sadness in her eyes. She had turned four children loose on the world, and here she was, forced to turn her fifth child loose as well.

It was move-in day for me at Illinois State, and I had the usual freshman mix of feelings: excitement, apprehension, a bit of sadness, and a lot of curiosity about what living away from home would be like. But mainly I was excited to be taking the next step to adulthood.

Mom could sense my bubbling enthusiasm, probably making it all the harder on her. While I was bouncing down the steps with pillows, clothes, books, and third-hand pieces of furniture (think bright orange, swiveling, nappy polyester living room chairs), Mom was coming to grips with the end of her daily usefulness and intimate involvement in my life. That had to sting a bit. Having now experienced this "leave the kid at college for the first time" three times as a parent, I have an appreciation for what she was going through.

"We're going to miss you, Tim," she said as she brushed some hair out of her eyes. The skin around her eyes was damp, primarily—I thought—from perspiration. But a few private tears might have been mixed in. Regardless, the moisture somehow made her look even sadder.

"I'll miss you, too, Mom," I said, touching her upper arm. "It'll be okay, though. I'll probably be home this weekend." I have to admit, it was nice knowing I was just a 45-minute drive from home. That made for an easy safety net as I transitioned into college life.

"Oh, really? That would be great. I'd love that."

"Might be good to stay at least a couple of weeks," Dad said out of the side of his mouth. I suspected this was an obligatory fatherly comment, the counterbalance to tearful, hopeful Mom. Dad wanted to ensure that that my transition to manhood wouldn't be disrupted by too many visits home.

My basement apartment began to slowly look a bit more like home. Not by any stretch the warm and inviting place I'd called home for 18 years, but workable. A mixture of old and new clothes in the closet, a few pictures from home on the dresser, a couple of tacky posters on the cement walls and my precious multi-piece stereo, positioned at the end of my bed. Other than the fact that this was a typical basement abode, circa 1950s, it would do. I'd been slow returning my housing contract earlier that year, so by the time August 1979 arrived, the freshman dorms at Illinois State University were full. Completely. So, we'd scrambled to find an alternative housing arrangement and a family with whom we had church connections said they had one spot of four left. Terrific, we'd take it! Sight unseen.

Two bedrooms each with two single beds, neither bedroom equipped with a door (the bedrooms had essentially been created out of a single larger room with the insertion of a partial dividing wall—more like somewhat separated living spaces than private rooms). The place did have one bathroom, featuring two sinks and a tiled shower. Thankfully, the bathroom did have a door. The living area had a beat-up black-and-white TV that got two channels pretty well and two channels with a fair amount of visual snow. A basic kitchen, with a few old pots and pans left by prior residents. Linoleum floors throughout. Cement block walls, painted in a faint shade of lime green. Four young males, none particularly skilled in the cleaning arts. Me, the lone underclassman, a neophyte among an experienced and worldly-wise "mentors." This was indeed a brave new world. And I could not have been happier.

Big Man on Campus? Not by a long shot. I was a typical, wide-eyed, fresh-faced freshman, completely naïve and eager with enthusiasm for whatever college could throw at me. The sense of liberation was palpable. Invigorating. Energizing. It was as if the crispness of the fall air filling my lungs on my bike rides into campus was enlivening both my physical and spiritual senses. I was alive in a way I'd never experienced before. This new life chapter had a lot of moving pieces, and it was marked most notably by lack of boundaries and rules. Don't want to eat tuna noodle casserole for dinner? No problem. Want to stay up until 2 a.m., with a pizza break at midnight? Check. Feeling like skipping a class and sleeping in? Well, now, there are certain lines I didn't want to cross!

In the exciting new world of unleashed college freshman, I was given the awesome opportunity (and now I recognize, privilege) to make my own way, to make choices that would impact the rest of my life. It was wondrous in so many ways. Two ways, in particular. One, it would prove to be a time of finding my way in faith, a way that was authentic and meaningful, and, at the same time, surrendered to God. Two, it would be a time of foundation-laying for my future as an entrepreneur. Neither of these profound directions was obvious, per se, that first year on the campus of Illinois State. But there were certainly hints of what lay ahead over the ensuing four years.

The entrepreneurial part of my development was keyed to my participation in the Student Accounting Society. I got heavily involved with SAS as a sophomore and remained so for the balance of my time at ISU. We held monthly meetings where speakers from accounting and consulting firms were invited to present some aspect of the professional accounting world to us (and to soft-sell the merits of joining their particular company upon graduation). SAS also featured about a dozen committees that members could get involved with. I was most involved with the Business Week committee, representing SAS in what was "the event" for the College of Business every year. Business Week featured social events, workshops, outside speakers, and was indeed the signature, celebratory event held each spring to educate, inspire, and inform business school students. Challenged by all that had to be done in connection with the role of SAS in Business Week, I had no choice but to plan, think, and act entrepreneurially. That, in turn, further whetted my appetite. I decided to run for SAS president, and I prepared a two-minute presentation to support my candidacy.

Each of the candidates for committee chair took their turns at the dais, explaining why they represented a solid choice for the position. Now, mind you, these were accounting students, not known for oratorical flourishes. So by the time Tammy Creason and I were to make our respective pitches for the office of president, the student crowd had grown pretty restless. That is, those who hadn't already nodded off.

Tammy went first. She sparkled in her two-minute pitch. That was going to be a tough act to follow. In fact, Tammy was so impressive that I decided it would be a good idea to ask her out on a date! (She said no.) I took my turn, and as I recall, did pretty well—but not well enough. The votes were tallied that evening, with Tammy announced as next year's SAS president.

Ah, my first taste of public defeat. Didn't feel great; actually felt downright awful. But I had a choice to make. Would I pout and sulk, or would I jump back in with resilience, remaining as active in SAS as ever? The choice, in fact, was easy—and would become a pattern for how I would interact with failure and defeat over the ensuing 30 years.

Over the next two years of my college life—playing a leadership role in SAS, interacting with partners from numerous outside accounting firms, engaging in outreach programs like bell ringing for the Salvation Army—a new vision of what my entrepreneurial future might hold began to take shape. As a youngster and pretty much until stepping foot onto the ISU campus, I had assumed I would go back to the family business to fulfill my entrepreneurial itch and play my dutiful role as the next generation taking over Hoerr Nursery. But as I fully embraced my "college education" (be it in the classroom, the café, or the pub), I began to imagine an alternative view of the future. What would it look like if I embraced a career as an accounting professional? What possibilities waited? What might I achieve? And, really, what was the risk?

And so I began writing a new script of what the future might be, and ultimately made the decision that at least a few years in the world of professional accounting made good sense. This script was a breakaway from the one that had been written—quite benevolently, I might add—by my parents and the larger system within which I was raised. Often these well-meaning scripts end up leading us along a path that is safer, more predictable, and certainly more suited to what others would have us do with our lives. Breaking away and writing a new vision of the future is not a trivial matter. As such, I might consider my authoring of the new script my first truly entrepreneurial act.

At the same time as this "entrepreneurial shift of thought" was occurring, I was experiencing a parallel dynamic in my spiritual walk. Things I had always assumed to be true about God were proving to be far less black and white. Most truth, I was learning, appeared to be paradoxical. The closer I got to the heart of an issue, the more complex and nuanced the "right" thing to do seemed. I had always thought that truth was obvious, that the Bible provided unequivocal guidance on most life issues, and that there was typically a "right answer" for most situations. One example, symbolic of the myriad other, typically smaller, ways I was encountering the complexity of spiritual truth, has stuck with me.

Jane was a member of our bible study group at ISU, which met on Thursday nights. She had graduated from nursing school a few years back, but lived in town and enjoyed hanging out with college students. Most of us did not know about the struggles Jane was having with depression. Only when she was admitted to the psychiatric care unit of the local hospital did most of our group become aware of her illness. Now, I'd come to believe that depression was something pretty black and white—more to the point, godly people were "immune" from this disease. I couldn't figure out why someone as vivacious as Jane had gone so far as to check herself in to the hospital. But as I learned more about Jane's difficult struggle—which had been going on for years, actually—I began to see that this was an extremely complicated issue that was anything but clear-cut. Ultimately coming to a much more sympathetic understanding of Jane's intense emotional, chemical, and spiritual battle, I felt foolish for my naïve, simplistic, and judgmental reduction of the matter.

This experience compelled me to ask questions I had not asked before. Who is God and what is the real nature of my relationship with him? How can I know what is really truth in any given set of circumstances? How do I discern the best way to align myself with the Creator, to discover and live out the calling on my life? So, just as the entrepreneurial theme of my life was newly emerging, the spiritual simplicity that I'd always embraced began to take on new dimensions and deeper explorations. I became unsatisfied with traditional answers to life's complex challenges, and pressed ever deeper into a personal relationship with God.

As part of this process, I began to explore other Christian traditions, with the growing realization that God had a pretty large tent. I visited many churches during this time—Baptist, independent, Evangelical Free, charismatic, and even Catholic. While several themes were common across all of these expressions of Christianity, I began to appreciate the differences, both subtle and obvious, as well as the varied points of emphasis from one to the other.

Christian rock concerts became standard fare for my cohorts and me, and I eagerly sought out teaching seminars such as the Bible Prophecy weekend and Walk Through the Bible seminar. My college years were ones of intense inquiry, deconstructing much of what I'd always assumed to be foundational truth, and reassembling a more robust, nuanced, and profound sense of faith. While this process entailed risk—and indeed, many who go down this path are unable to reach the reassembly stage—somehow I never lost the sense of the Spirit's careful touch throughout. And as I experienced that touch—simultaneously delicate yet powerful—I was discovering a variety of unexpected answers to the question I'd begun to ask years earlier: "Who is Jesus?"

10. Big City Kid

Chicago, Illinois
February 1983

THE SCORE WAS 2-1 CHICAGO BLACKHAWKS. It was the intermission between the second and third periods, and the new team slogan, produced through a fan contest, had just been announced: "The Hawks will, Hawks will, rock you." A wild chorus of boos rained down from the arena. Not original enough? Too simple? I couldn't figure out why everyone was so angry. The fans did not like it, and they were vocally expressing their displeasure. The boos grew louder. And louder. The announcer could no longer be heard. A few pieces of concession trash had been flung onto the ice. Suffice it to say that this particular slogan was probably short-lived. Welcome to the world of professional ice hockey and a rabid fan base unlike any other.

As a youngster, I'd been to Wrigley Field to take in a few baseball games. In my college years, I'd become a loyal Illinois State Redbird fan, attending sold-out games at the Horton Fieldhouse. But none of those experiences had prepared me for my inaugural experience with pro hockey. A rock and roll atmosphere, fueled by consumption of adult beverages. Numerous fights between fans in the seats—mirroring a number of fights on the ice. (Or perhaps the fights on the ice mirrored the fights in the stands?) A profuse amount of spicy language.

"Pretty cool, huh?" Matt Brown (not his real name) said. Matt, an Arthur Andersen manager, leaned over and nudged me in the ribs.

"Uh, yeah, I guess you could say that," I managed.

"Ever been to a pro hockey game before?" he asked, knowing full well by the expression on my face that I was a pro hockey newbie.

"No, can't say that I have."

"Well, this is just one of the neat parts of working for the world's biggest and best accounting firm, Tim. Get used to it. You're in for quite a ride." Matt smiled.

We were sitting fairly close to center ice, maybe 15 rows up. Pretty sweet seats. And, as Matt pointed out, just one of the perks of working for Arthur Andersen, the premier firm in the world at that time. Although I was just an intern, 1 of 13 seniors in accounting from Illinois State University, I was being baptized into a corporate culture as unique and peculiar as the hockey game experience. Dinners at the best restaurants in the Chicago Loop. A weeklong, all-expenses-paid training session at the lovely St. Charles-based educational center (particularly good cherry pie, as I recall). Business cards with my name on them, the first day in the office! All of that and 60- to 70-hour workweeks to boot (we were spared no part of the authentic experience).

I had to admit, this was a pretty heady experience for a 21-year-old from the industrial river town of Peoria. Commuting to the gorgeous downtown office via train. Flagging down a taxi to whisk me to my next client engagement. Walking the streets of the Windy City, with the chill of winter invigorating and inviting me to accept the challenge of this new and exciting life. Other than extremely long work hours, limited time for family, friends, and life beyond the friendly confines of Arthur Andersen, what was there not to like? So at the end of the three-month internship in early 1983, it was decision time. An offer of full-time employment had been extended to each of the interns from ISU. One of my accounting major colleagues and close friends, Clark Ribordy, had already accepted the offer. We were back on the ISU campus by that time, and I asked Clark to meet me for lunch at the Garcia's Pizza in a Pan behind Watterson Towers.

"Tim, this is a once in a lifetime opportunity," Clark said as he bit into a slice of Gutbuster. "This is the pinnacle of our lives to this point."

"No doubt, Clark. There are a lot of things I really like about this deal, but...."

"But...?" Clark raised an eyebrow. "But what, Tim? No question as far as I'm concerned. Are you seriously thinking of taking another offer?"

"Well, no," I said as I sipped some soda. "Uh, well, yes. I mean, I don't know. I'm struggling on this one. I need to know if this is part of the bigger plan for my life—whether it's really the best fit for me at this point."

"Bigger plan? What does that mean? It doesn't get any bigger than Arthur Andersen, my friend. Case closed!"

Over the next couple of weeks, I learned that all of the interns had accepted the offer from Arthur Andersen—everyone but me. I'd also been offered a job in Champaign with the local office of McGladrey & Pullen, a relatively large regional firm at the time. A job was also waiting at a Peoria-based firm (my parents' choice of the three!). For some reason, I felt a tug on my heart toward the opportunity in Champaign. It didn't make a lot of sense, to be frank. AA was the top accounting firm in the world, and I would be working for their flagship office in the city that also housed their world headquarters. And the city that was home to my favorite baseball team, the Chicago Cubs! The opportunities for advancement would be unlimited. I could certainly see myself progressing to becoming a partner with AA. The vision was powerful, palpable, compelling.

The Champaign firm was much smaller, but it too had a certain appeal. Ron Bates and Terry Snyder, my two key points of contact there, had both spent time at large firms, so they empathized with my situation. They also sweetened their deal by offering me the potential to build a career in a relatively new discipline for accounting firms at the time—management consulting. I would start as an auditor, but if I showed sufficient progress, I'd be offered a transfer into this exciting new division.

Facing big decisions like this is, of course, the norm for college seniors. Making major life decisions at that point in one's life is, in fact, the point! But nothing in my life had prepared me for the enormity and complexity of that decision. Nothing except a sense that God had called me to himself and that he had prepared me in advance for this moment—and that I deeply desired to select the option that somehow fit into that framework. But what did that really mean, in practical terms? Listing the pros and cons? Putting the features and benefits into some sort of mental, emotional weighing device? Where did the spiritual element fit in? How could I know which of these paths would best lead me to the fulfillment of God's call on my life? That was really the crux of the matter for me, and it was then that I turned to my brother Ben, who had become a pastor at the Vineyard Church in Urbana, Illinois, a church that was, shall I say, quite a bit more progressive in its theology, liturgy, and practice than the one we grew up in.

Most of the conversations took place over the phone, as I was fairly consumed time-wise with the crash prep course for the CPA exam. I explained my dilemma to Ben. He listened carefully, articulating back to me what he heard me saying. He didn't seem to be in a rush with specific advice; it seemed for him to be more about the process and getting me to open up my heart.

"I don't think there is a blueprint that you're to follow, Tim," Ben said. "It's more about a blank canvas waiting to be painted."

"Well, that certainly injects some freedom into the equation, but it also makes it more challenging in a sense," I said.

"I agree. That's the cool thing about discovering God's will in choosing something as important as a career and a place to live," Ben said. Even over the phone, I could tell he was smiling as he said this. "Sometimes, God might have an optimal choice for us. Other times, perhaps not. But he wants us to earnestly seek him in the process, enjoy the journey of making the decision, and then wait for his leading."

"But what does that leading look like, Ben? I mean, really. I don't have any experience in this kind of thing. The closest parallel was deciding a major for college, and Dad pretty well mapped that one out for me!"

"It's usually a combination of things that end up resonating with one another," Ben said. "Wise counsel from others. A scripture that resonates with you. Maybe a vivid dream. Ultimately, it comes down to a settled peace with the choice you're making. That's the best you can do."

And for the next couple of weeks, I wrestled, prayed, and talked with Ben two or three more times. The clarity just wasn't coming easily. And the peer pressure seemed to be mounting. Others looking in were sure of the right choice—and in nearly every case, that meant taking the Andersen job in Chicago. Ever been in a situation where everyone else seems to know what you should do? "Okay, that's what I'll do," I told myself one night as I weighed the pros and cons of my two job offers. "I'll take the AA job. Case closed, as Clark said a month ago."

But once I made the decision, the emotional wrestling only got worse. I couldn't sleep. Normally a starving college student, food held no interest. I was, to put it bluntly, an emotional mess. What gives? I thought. Everyone else seems to know the right choice in this deal but me. Maybe I'm not supposed to go to Chicago after all.

And at that moment, I heard a still, small voice gently inviting me to make "a more authentic choice"—the choice to go to Champaign and take the position with McGladrey. And that's what I did. I switched train tracks in my heart and immediately felt a sense of settled peace—aha!—the very thing Ben had said was most important in the whole process. And with that peace come a growing sense of excitement. "Champaign, here I come!" I exclaimed to myself.

This turned out to be a decision that would lead me on a most unexpected journey. I thought I'd made only a career decision; but I'd underestimated the impact that the move would have on every aspect of my life. One of the most obvious and impactful—and delightful—surprises was just around the corner.

I hadn't dated much in high school or college—maybe one or two semi-serious relationships that lasted about two months. I suppose it was combination of being raised in a religious system that looked down on that sort of thing, along with a laser-beam focus on academics that left little time for an amorous relationship. All the while, I enjoyed great fun with guys and girls alike, just hanging out and experiencing life together. But within weeks of arriving in Champaign, a particular member of the opposite gender had caught my attention—serious attention.

Toni McIntyre had moved to Champaign only a year or so earlier. Months before I relocated, I had visited the church that my brother and brother-in-law were co-pastoring—and Toni and I were introduced to each other at the back of the church by my five year old nephew, Jonathan Leman. While Toni can recall several specifics from that first meeting, including the clothes I was wearing and what was said, my memory of it was and is fairly cloudy. Typical male. Something must have been sparked, though.

After moving to Champaign in July of 1983, I was quickly becoming "interested" in Toni. In the month of October, things began to heat up—and downright boil over. Toni and I, along with a few others from the "young adults group" went bowling one night. She had the strangest little hop just before releasing the bowling ball—and the cutest little laugh that went with it. *I think I am really falling for her*, I thought to myself. The following week, we found ourselves sharing a hay bale on what turned out to be the world's longest hayrack ride (the tractor driver got lost in a big way in rural Champaign County). A week later, we were official. And, um, a month or so after that, we were engaged. The only way I can describe this whirlwind, happy zaniness was "it was a God thing." While I hadn't previously been on the lookout for a relationship, the most amazing woman had come crashing into my world—and I wasn't about to let her go. By June of the following year, we were married (and just last month, we celebrated 30 years!).

11. Called

Champaign, Illinois
July 4 1983

WITH THE FIREWORKS EXPLODING OVERHEAD, I laid my head back in the soft grass. The quintessential sights and sounds of Independence Day surrounded me. Little kids with sparklers. Moms and dads shooting off Roman candles. Picnic dinners spread out on blankets. This was Americana at its best! Only a few days prior, I had unloaded all of my worldly possessions, mostly hand-me-down furniture from Mom and Dad, into the apartment on Valley Road in Champaign, just across from Hessel Park. The following week, I would start my professional accounting career. The celebration around me resonated with the emotions I was feeling that evening—a new era of freedom had arrived, a whole new future awaited, and I was up for it!

McGladrey was pretty much everything I had hoped for in a starting position. Challenging work. Engaging colleagues. A sense of significance as I transitioned from college student to the working world. And true to their word, Terry Snyder and Ron Bates, my primary contacts at McGladrey, offered me a transfer to the exciting world of management consulting at about the six-month mark of my career.

The work got even more interesting from that point forward. Microcomputers were the hot new thing—particularly something called the Compaq luggable. It was a microcomputer the size of a large Samsonite suitcase, weighing about 40 pounds, with a tiny little display screen about 8 inches across. It ran a cool little software program called Lotus 1-2-3, along with a handful of other things. Recognizing the power of this newfangled thing called an "electronic spreadsheet," I was soon building financial projections, net present value models, and all other sorts of financial analyses for anyone and everyone in the firm. I became known as "the doctor." If you had a problem that could be solved with a spreadsheet, I would heal your pain!

The work was fulfilling and the challenges were new every week. I almost felt guilty that I was being paid to do something that I really enjoyed. That being the case, I was even more excited about the preparation my job was giving me for what I thought was my "real calling." The first two to three years of my career coincided with a pretty powerful spiritual awakening in me—a sort of "next step" from the period of intense inquiry I'd undergone in college.

I was encountering God-moments on a routine basis. These were everyday occurrences that seemed to me to have the fingerprint of God on them. For example, because I was cutting new territory in working with computers and spreadsheets, I would often run into complex problems for which no precedent existed. No one in the firm could help me. There was no Internet to Google the list of solutions. So, I would typically pray over these problems and ask for specific wisdom on how to resolve them. Soon, I would often have the answer on a practical approach to take. Others in the office were taking note of this, particularly the partners. That led to receiving more complicated assignments, and I found myself double-booked on more than one occasion.

In parallel to my progress in the workplace, I was seeing great truths leap and grab me from the pages of scripture like never before. Though I had grown up attending Sunday school, I had understood scripture to be mostly interesting background material for moral living. The "characters" in the stories seemed stuck on that Sunday school flannel board.

But here I was reading verses in Psalms and Ephesians, for example, which seemed so pertinent to the work and life situations I was encountering. I found myself laughing out loud at how well different scripture readings had just the nugget I needed for a situation happening at work!

Most likely because of being in this state of heightened spiritual awareness, I assumed that the invitation to leave the accounting/consulting world to enter into God's "real" calling was imminent. All of these God moments and spiritual phenomena were certainly indicators that something big was about to happen. I recall a conversation with one of my McGladrey supervisors, Dan Brooks, which occurred as we worked together on an out-of-town assignment in Evansville, Indiana. We were working through a couple of thick steaks at the Sirloin Stockade.

"So, Tim, you seem to be doing pretty well here at McGladrey," Dan said as he cut into his T-bone steak. "If I had to predict, I'd say you have a pretty good shot at making partner in the firm, and at the least, being promoted rapidly through the ranks."

"Thanks, Dan. I'm enjoying being here, to be sure. I really like the work and the people. But I'm pretty sure my time here is temporary," I said as I took a bite of my baked potato.

"Temporary? Are you looking for another job already? Why would you do that?"

"Oh, no, I'm not looking to take another job. It's not that at all. It's just that I sense I'll be doing some kind of ministry work relatively soon."

Dan looked puzzled. "Ministry work. Like a missionary?"

"Well, that's one option," I said. "Pastoral work is another one. Or maybe Bible translation for an unreached people group."

"Unreached people group? What are you talking about? You seem to speaking a different language, pal."

"Oh. Sorry. I guess that's too much 'Christian-ese' there. What I'm trying to say is, this public accounting gig is great, but I have a sense of calling to do something big for God. And, any day now, I expect to get some clarity on just exactly what that calling will look like at a practical level. But I'm pretty sure it means I'll have to leave McGladrey in order to do it."

Dan chewed on a piece of meat for a minute, not sure how to respond. "Hmm. Leaving McGladrey because the Big Man Upstairs is calling you to something big. So, how do you expect to get this clarity? Do you actually hear God speaking to you?"

"Not in the way you and I are talking. But I do expect that God will somehow show me the steps I'm supposed to take to fulfill my real calling. Just not quite sure what that will look like, but I should know it when I see it!" I declared with confidence, as a piece of blue cheese from my salad dribbled off my chin and on to my tie.

From my first days in the professional world, I was eagerly on the lookout for God showing up and pointing me in a new direction of full-time ministry. At the same time, I was committed to doing my consulting job with excellence. It was an interesting tension to manage, but manage it I did. I knew that the anticipation of my "real calling" should not in any way cause me to disrespect the work at hand—and so I put my shoulder to the wheel and worked all the harder.

In 1985, an opportunity did present itself to leave McGladrey for another position with a consulting company founded and run by Scott Reichard, a good friend of mine from the Vineyard Church. Because of the church connection and Scott's vision to grow the company's service offerings to include some of my specialty areas, I decided to give the opportunity very serious consideration. In some strange way, I decided it was a decent stepping-stone to an imminent ministry calling, perhaps because Scott and I really connected at a spiritual level, in particular sharing a worldview of integrating faith and work. Maybe Scott could move me along the path to ministry more effectively, I thought. In short order, I took the position and got to work.

About a year and half later, with the workload primarily concentrated on service areas outside my bailiwick and feeling a bit in over my head, I sensed that I had probably taken a detour. I wasn't any closer to moving into ministry, and I would say that I seemed to be regressing professionally. So I floated an inquiry to the partners at McGladrey about returning there. They were eager to have me back, which was a pleasant surprise.

Returning to the accounting firm after being exposed to a situation that was out of alignment for me gave me a new urgency and crisp focus in my work. The benefit of being out of sync for the previous year and half yielded surprisingly good fruit in my return to the consulting group at McGladrey. In fact, within a year of my return, I was promoted to manager, a mid-level position with the firm that came with a few perks and more importantly, the opportunity to supervise a team. That was a challenge that I relished. Although I had proved myself a competent do-bee, I hadn't shown much capacity for replicating my skills in others and leading a team. It was time to get after my new assignment! Indeed, for the next few years, I worked hard at building my interpersonal and leadership skills, while improving my technical skills as well. I figured I'd need both sets to take advantage of new opportunities down the road—whether in business or ministry.

And then the moment I'd been waiting for arrived. Spring of 1989. The Vineyard Church Small Group Leader Retreat at McCormick's Creek State Park in Indiana. Toni and I had been leading small groups for six years at that point, a role we really enjoyed. Encouraging singles and young couples in the midst of life's challenges was one of the key factors in strengthening our own marriage and family, which now featured two young daughters—Alyssa, 4, and Audra, 1. The small group leader retreat was an annual event designed to reward and refresh the volunteer leadership corps of the church. It was a time of hanging out together, worshipping, trail walking, eating together, playing games, and being encouraged by the pastoral staff.

For a couple of reasons, I sensed that God would be showing up at this retreat with a summons for me—that it was once-and-for-all time to take the leap of faith into the real calling he had for me. For one thing, I'd been working at my professional career for nearly six years, which was longer than I had anticipated. For another, I had a remarkable dream on the Wednesday evening preceding the retreat.

In the dream, I found myself in Terminal D of Lambert—St. Louis International Airport. Terminal D was one of several used by TWA Airlines, the airline I typically used out of Champaign for both business and personal travel. In the dream, I stood in a boarding line at gate D-

25, and I distinctly remember thinking I hope I am able to board in time for this flight to St. Louis. I absolutely need to make it to St. Louis tonight. Strange thing was, I was already in St. Louis. Dreams can be a little odd that way, of course. The next thing I noticed was the sign behind the counter agent indicated a destination of Cincinnati. Well, that was also strange. I was trying to make a flight to St. Louis, while standing in the boarding line for Cincinnati. I remember a feeling of confusion, a sense of "what do I do now?"

And, then I awoke abruptly, sweating and shaking. This was no ordinary dream. I had had plenty of those in my 27 years. This was unmistakably some kind of message, and it was resonating deeply in me. I was simply unable to dismiss the dream as ordinary. It was far too vivid, gripping, real. The dream seemed to be Part A of God getting my attention leading into the retreat, and I was looking forward to experiencing Part B! But try as I might, I couldn't make sense of the dream. If there was a deeper meaning, it was escaping me.

When Toni and I checked in to the lovely wood-and-stone park lodge, it was mid-afternoon on a Thursday. We were one of the earlier arrivals, with the scheduled events starting after dinner that evening. We proceeded to our room for a little catnap. Welcoming us was a nice little basket of goodies—fruit, nuts, a couple of candy bars, bottled water—and two retreat T-shirts. Very cool. This weekend felt special already. Whenever God wants to show up and spell out Part B is fine with me, but I would prefer it sooner than later, I thought.

We rested for about an hour and were awakened by a phone call from my brother-in-law, Happy Leman, the senior pastor of our church. He invited us to join the pastoral staff for dinner. Perhaps this would be it. Maybe over dinner, Hap will extend an offer to join the Vineyard pastoral staff! We eagerly agreed to join for dinner, and I turned to Toni and said, "Are you ready for a life-changing dinner tonight? This could be a tipping point for us."

She seemed a little skeptical or apprehensive. As enthused as I was about some impending call to ministry, Toni was grounded in the more practical elements of making a comfortable and secure home for our two daughters. Exactly how my notion of the life-changing call to ministry fit in, she wasn't sure. In fact, the odds were pretty good that she preferred the stability of the McGladrey job!

Dinner was delightful. Engaging conversation. Lots of laughter. A sense of anticipation of the others arriving. But there was no mention of a job offer. And no hint of any message from God as to a Part B. I did, however, share my dream with my sister Dianne, Happy's wife and co-senior pastor of the church. Dianne and I had basically grown up in different households with little relationship between us, she being about 12 years older than me. But subsequent to my move to Champaign in 1983, we really enjoyed rekindling a delightful sibling relationship. We enjoyed regular discussions on the latest books we'd read, and we shared a deep interest in the more mystical elements of the Christian faith. As I shared with Dianne that evening, I did little to contextualize the dream, not wanting to lead her on in any particular direction. She agreed to ponder and pray over it, to see if something came to mind. That evening, as the retreat got formally underway with the other volunteer small group leaders, the sense of God's presence was strong. I went to bed that evening encouraged, albeit no more clear about the future than I'd started the day.

The next morning at breakfast, Di ran up to me with a big smile on her face. Almost giddy with excitement, she shared that God had showed her a pretty clear interpretation of the crazy dream I'd shared with her the night before. I was all ears! She proceeded to say that she sensed I was struggling with a major decision (true, though she did not know that!), and that the dream was very much about that decision. Check. She then said, "You are waiting on something—as illustrated by being in the boarding line at the airport. But God wants you to know that you are already where you are supposed to be. You are in a 'saintly' place—as represented by being in the St. Louis airport. You are wrestling with getting to St. Louis without realizing that you are indeed already there." Hmmm. That really jolted me, but at the same time, it excited me. "Furthermore," she said, "to make a change—to go somewhere other than where you presently are—would be a 'sin' (Cincinnati)—as evidenced by the destination sign at the airport gate."

Wow. I took a step backwards, my body feeling as if someone had physically grabbed hold of me and pushed. Di's interpretation made a lot of sense to me. But it went far beyond a mental assent of what she was saying. As my body reacted, my emotions and inner spirit joined in, too. Was I indeed "already where I was really called to be"? Could I have been mistaken for the last six years, thinking that the real calling was something more spiritual, more holy than the position I held with McGladrey?

I felt a wave of peace and a powerful energy come over me. The tightly-held paradigm of what it meant to be called by God was breaking off of me, like chunks of concrete. With the debris of the old way of thinking now at my feet, a new freedom was coming, a new understanding was dawning. It was indeed a high calling, a most spiritual calling—yes, my real calling—to be the most excellent businessperson I could be. To embrace the small domain of my team of colleagues, my clients and their problems, and fully deploy my skills, expertise, and my passion in meeting needs in a godly and most excellent way.

That revelation was a bigger bombshell than if Dianne had told me to pack my bags and head to Africa to live out the rest of my days as a missionary.

The rest of that weekend offered up one confirmation after another that God's Part B was calling me to not only stay put, but to fully thrive right where I was! A noontime conversation with the youth pastor, Hank Sanford, and his wife Marla, offered fresh affirmation that I was doing in my career what I was supposed to be doing. Ben's presentation that evening conveyed a similar point. The songs we sang at Friday evening's worship settled it once and for all. Could this all have been a strange coincidence? The odds were against it.

Indeed, as the weekend drew to a close, I knew beyond knowing that God had appointed me to continue growing, developing, and serving others in the business world. I showed up at work that Monday with an amazing new perspective on my work. Not that I had been previously sloughing off, but somehow having the weight of a crooked and dysfunctional paradigm lifted off me was releasing a whole new energy I had not previously experienced.

As 1989 proceeded to unfold, I received a promotion to senior manager, a highly selective designation that puts one on the short track to partner. The promotion was an exclamation point to the process of embracing the new truth that my calling to the world of business was legit.

More importantly, I began embrace the truth that everyone is called, not just those serving in traditional ecclesiastical or ministry positions. Furthermore, it began to dawn on me that nearly all human beings would discover and live out callings in settings far removed from those deemed by society as religious or spiritual. While mine was in the milieu of business, others would find theirs in the world of the arts, others in science, some in homemaking, and others in politics or entertainment.

You see, God is concerned with saving, or setting right, the entire world of people, nations, institutions, ideas, and things—and that's a pretty big job. He's not just seeking to "save" individuals; the scope of the project is much bigger than that. It encompasses the whole of creation. Now, he could choose to do this project on his own, and I'm not altogether sure why he doesn't. But the fact is, he chooses human beings to execute the plan of restoring the entire created order to one of peace, joy, and beauty. And the encouraging news is, we are all chosen to participate in this grand project. People in every conceivable vocation and walk of life—the arts, sciences, religion, education, business, government, entertainment, indeed all of society—are needed to fulfill the magnificent scope of God's restoration project.

As I began to apprehend just a glimpse of this wonderful truth, my work was imbued with a deeper sense of meaning and purpose. Not only was I motivated to be productive in the immediate tasks at hand, but I felt compelled to become a student of how God's grand project worked, to determine how I could best play a role in it. It also meant that I brought an attitude of eager learner to my work assignments—knowing that the implications of work well done were far beyond just the local sphere in which the work activities took place. Lastly, I was determined to become a teacher of what I learned by embodying this powerful truth and leading others into this "new way."

12. Cracking the Code to Become a Leader

Champaign, Illinois
November 1988

ONE OF THE THINGS THAT I REALLY APPRECIATE about my tenure at McGladrey was the opportunity to make a transition from do-bee to manager/leader, with a tremendous amount of "scaffolding and support." While I made plenty of mistakes along the way, the firm and its partners were encouraging and helpful. For those of us trained in a technical discipline like accounting, engineering, or law, this can be a tough slog. Competence in the technical discipline is not a predictor of success as a manager or leader of technicians!

I faced two challenges in particular. One was some initially discouraging feedback about my leadership potential from a battery of tests I took and the other was the Code 71 paradox (I'll explain this paradox later in this chapter). Both of these roadblocks had to be dealt with and overcome. And this process was no small factor in readying me for the world of entrepreneurship, where one wears many hats but most notably must be a leader of people and a manager of productivity.

The first challenge sprang from a series of tests I took in connection with my role as a small group leader at the Vineyard Church. The church wanted to help its volunteer leadership team to become more effective, and that process started with a collection of testing instruments—Meyers-Briggs, DiSC, the Minnesota Multiphasic Personality Inventory, and the like. A professional mental health firm was hired to administer the tests and interpret the results, with the basic goal being to "increase each leader's awareness of his or her strengths, blind spots, and areas for continued development." Fair enough.

I actually enjoyed the process of taking the tests and in fact looked forward to the feedback. I wasn't prepared, though, for being run over by a semi. Sitting at my desk at work, I read through the results of each individual test, not particularly noting anything unusual. There were some interesting tidbits, some good, and some bad. Nothing seemed too far off what I had expected. But then I flipped to the final couple of pages in the feedback packet. There, Dr. Green (not his real name) had prepared a customized and rather personal summary of "the bigger story" he had determined was being told by the combination of the various test results. He proceeded to lay out an interesting case, the bottom line of which was "Tim is clearly not leadership material at this stage—perhaps a 2 out of 5 at best—and he will require a significant amount of work in order to overcome his deficiencies." BAM!

I had certainly expected some things to work on, but nothing had prepared me for this conclusion. I pushed my chair back from my desk, reeling. What did that mean? Hadn't I already proven myself as a leader? Wasn't I, in fact, leading a group of professionals at work, while leading a small group at church—and hopefully leading my family, to boot? But in black and white, Dr. Green had declared me a "leadership wannabe," an incompetent.

Driving home after receiving this news, I remember a feeling of incredible bewilderment. Toni greeted me at the door with her usual warm smile and a big hug. She must have known I needed that.

"Honey, can you read this summary page for me?" I asked, a bit sheepishly, noticeably shaking.

"Sure. What's the deal? You look white as a ghost." Toni looked a bit worried.

"Well, I don't want to color your thinking before you read it. Just take a look and let me know what you think."

Toni read the summary, her eyes widening as she neared the end. "Wow. That's some conclusion. Where did he come up with that?"

"That's what I thought, but I wanted to make sure it wasn't just me seeing this from my biased perspective."

"The interesting thing is, you've been a small group leader at church for eight years or so—and you've been promoted a couple of times at McGladrey. You've taken on some larger roles with the national firm, too. Aren't those indications that you have at least some emerging leadership skills?" Toni was clearly growing agitated, echoing the sentiments I had thought immediately after reading Dr. Green's assessment.

"What do you think of running this by Ben?" I said. I trusted my brother's judgment, and wanted to know what he thought.

"Good idea—see if he thinks this is a fair rendition or not. He's usually pretty balanced on these kinds of things."

Ben and I got together at a café the following Tuesday morning to talk over coffee. In advance, I'd given him a copy of the psychologist's report.

"I can certainly see why you're upset, Tim," he said. "That's a pretty bold conclusion that doesn't seem too well supported by the actual test results. It's a disconnect, if you ask me."

"Well, that's what I thought," I said. "I certainly see there are some things to work on, but his conclusion seemed a bit out in left field."

"Well, there are some nuggets of truth here, but I think you should give little weight to Dr. Green's overall conclusion. Do you think you can differentiate between the two?" Ben asked.

"I don't know, frankly. I think I can, but it's tough," I said. "I'd like to throw the whole thing out. But I agree with you, there are some worthwhile pieces of feedback in here. I just can't embrace the '2 out of 5 serious deficiencies' thing."

"If it helps, you should know that this is one person's judgment. Yes, he is a professional. But professionals do sometimes get it wrong. Or, they can see things from a very different angle than you or me. Consider figure skating and gymnastics judges—the same professionals watching the same competition can offer very different assessments of what they saw. Perhaps that's the case here," Ben said.

"Thanks. That does help. I'm asking God to illuminate the pearls, as you are suggesting—but help me to not throw out the baby with the bathwater."

Over the next few weeks, I was able to see more of the pearls that were included in the feedback report from Dr. Green's summary. I needed to narrow my focus and eliminate some things from my plate. I needed to be more sensitive to coming across as a prima donna to others (I thought exuding confidence was a good thing!). And I needed to become a more patient person. All good things pointed out in Dr. Green's report—and pretty much on the mark. At the same time, the collective wisdom from Toni, Ben, and a handful of others helped me to see that Dr. Green might have missed the central point—that I did indeed have the basic package from which a leader could be made. As I wrestled through this raw, soul-searching process, I was able to conclude that I could indeed become a good leader and that while Dr. Green was entitled to his view, I didn't have to accept this assessment as ironclad and unchangeable.

So, while I was able to climb outside of Dr. Green's box and begin to implement some of the changes outlined above, I faced another, more practical challenge: Code 71.

Well, not the code literally, but what it represented. Code 71 was one of several timekeeping codes that we accountants used to track our time. Twice a month, each professional in the firm was required to submit a timesheet so that clients could be properly charged for the work done and management could track overall productivity. This rather chaotic exercise was humorously visible in changed behavior patterns on "timesheet day"(the deadline required for submission). Some of us would assemble our timesheet from Post-It notes and scraps of paper scattered throughout our offices, others would use the approach of recopying numbers out of neatly kept Day-Timers, and some of us resorted to creative memory reconstruction in the quest of a reasonable facsimile of the previous couple of weeks' chargeable time. It was, of course, the 1980s and those nifty electronic timesheets had yet to be invented (and for those of you under 50, Day-Timer was a brand of personal diary/calendar useful for tracking appointments and to-do lists).

One of the key principles of timekeeping was to allocate one's time into "billable" and "non-billable" activities. The billable actions were those charged to specific clients, resulting in revenue for the accounting firm. The non-billable activities included administrative work (like filling out a timesheet!), business development work (seeking new clients), going to the bathroom, drinking coffee with associates and training on new developments in the accounting world. Each of these non-billable activities had a category code associated with it, so you could enter non-billable time in the right manner.

Code 71 was one such non-billable code, and it was labeled "Personnel." When I first joined the firm, I wondered what this code really meant. After all, "personnel" seemed pretty nondescript—vague, you might say. This code wasn't covered in my orientation. And after that, no one said much about it. I figured it had some practical use for someone—but as a newbie accountant, I had little time to be concerned about "personnel" issues of any kind other than my own.

For the first several years of my accounting career, there was very little need to code any of my non-billable time to Code 71. I was there to crank out the work, and charge as much of it as possible to the "billable" categories on my timesheet. In fact, if you strayed too far from charging a certain percentage of your time to billable activities, you received a visit from the firm's managing partner, Lowell Garner. Lowell was a weathered and seasoned accounting pro, grandfatherly in appearance, but intimidating to the younger CPAs. While I later came to appreciate Lowell's unique manner and teddy-bear persona, I was scared to death of him for at least two or three years after joining the firm.

Why was there such emphasis on billable time? Because, accounting firms earn revenues (and ultimately, profits) based on time billed to clients, not on time spent in non-billable activities like administration, daydreaming, and bathroom breaks. But as I progressed in my career, I began to suspect there was a problem afoot with all of this emphasis on billable time. Indeed, there was a conundrum—a big catch-22. To really advance within the accounting firm, you had to learn how to delegate work to others—to "leverage" your time by allowing other professionals to handle the "do-bee" work, while you become a manager, handling multiple clients and projects simultaneously. To really be effective at managing, in other words delegating and leveraging, you had to spend time with your people. You had to spend time listening to them, developing them, inspiring them, encouraging them, and training them—and as a result, spending less time in directly billable activities. All of this "people time" was to be entered on one's timesheet as (you guessed it) Code 71.

Now, I was a pretty good do-bee, but I had less of a clue how to become a good manager and leader of others. I had some basic leadership skills, and Dr. Green's assessment aside, a foundation of confidence that leadership was my destiny. Still, spending time in Code 71 with my direct reports felt awkward to me—sort of like a shoe that didn't quite fit right. Besides, it was hard! Debits and credits, financial spreadsheets, computer software, I got. Dealing with a staffer's inability to work out an accounting problem, or his lack of focus due to fighting with his girlfriend the night before—or heaven forbid, why he was consistently late to work—was unfamiliar territory for me. Perhaps as challenging as anything, and really the crux of the Code 71 paradox, was that the more time I spent in Code 71 with my staff, the less time I was able to charge to billable activities. That particular statistic got noticed pretty much every two weeks, and was an essential component of one's performance evaluation and compensation.

Somehow, and in some way, I was able to grasp the essential truth that I would never progress in my career until I learned how to become a leader of others, reflected by the amount of time and effort spent in Code 71. I knew there would likely be some short-term cost to this activity that largely had to do with longer-term results. And accountants like short-term results! So as difficult as this was, I was determined to master the art of Code 71, with the goal of personally progressing while helping others progress. I wasn't going to use the excuse of not knowing how to do this, or the excuse of its degree of difficulty—I was determined to figure this out!

I began to reach out to the successful partners in the firm and ask (more like demand!) that they share with me the secrets of becoming a successful leader. If they weren't going to volunteer the information, then I would coax it out of them. I also began to rekindle my love for reading (I thought I had gotten rid of that "chore" once I earned my degree). I got my hands on as many leadership development books as I could find—sometimes reading as many as five or six at one time. I enrolled in experiential learning classes to develop skills that I didn't possess—the firm offered a few of these through its continuing education catalog, and others I sourced on my own. I distinctly remember successfully lobbying Mike Martin, my immediate superior partner, to attend the Creative Leadership seminar at Walt Disney World because it was a unique offering that I couldn't find anywhere else. And, perhaps as important as anything else, I began to actively look outside the firm to friends and mentors who could help me become the leader I had a vision of becoming.

To be honest, from about 1985 to 1992 was a pretty difficult time over which I learned some of the basics in the art of being a leader. It meant doubling up on the time I needed to invest in my career—time to work on client projects, time to learn about leadership, and time invested in those on my team so that they could become top performers. Not that I stopped there, of course. That was really only the beginning—a sort of "foundation laying," if you will, that set the stage for the rest of my career. Indeed, the topic of leadership has continued to be one of my lifelong passions—how to be the most effective leader I can be and how to best equip and inspire others in this same quest. It has meant a continual learning process and one that involves getting out of my comfort zone on a routine basis. To be honest, I'm not sure I've completely mastered the Code 71 paradox. But I'm continuing to work at cracking the code.

13. Czech Mate—New Game

Prague, Czechoslovakia
May 1992

THE SYMPHONY OF SMELLS DRIFTING OUR WAY FROM THE KITCHEN was delightful. Our seating arrangement in the living room was cozy. The small apartment was fixed up nicely, in traditional Czech décor, but was just a bit on the tiny side to be hosting four guests. The generosity of our hosts had not gone unnoticed. That they would agree to be our providers of room and board for a week was no small sacrifice for this young couple.

"Peter, I can't wait to see what you've cooked up. Tim looks like he's drooling in the corner over there," John Chisholm said. John was the team leader of our 1992 outreach trip to Czechoslovakia, which would become the Czech Republic and the Slovak Republic within seven months of our stay. John was one of the pastors at our local church, the Vineyard of Champaign-Urbana. Our church had joined forces with other Vineyard churches to assemble an outreach mission of assisting our brothers and sisters in this country with a rich history stretching back over centuries.

"If the meal tastes half as good as it smells, it will be amazing," I said. And, yes, I was drooling. Finally regaining my sense of hunger after bouts of nausea during the flight to Frankfort and the bus ride to Prague, I was absolutely famished. Several other members of our team seemed to be in a similar state.

"Well, I am sure you will enjoy it! I've made all of my favorites tonight!" Peter exclaimed, a big smile emerging from his behind his beard.

For the next two hours, our party of six—our two Czech hosts and four Americans—reveled in enthusiastic conversation around the meal of pork chops, seasoned potatoes, and red cabbage. Accompanied by dark, dense bread and a local Czech beer, it was the perfect end to our hectic day in Prague. And what made it so special was the fact that Peter had made everything from scratch.

"So you have just finished a very traditional Czech meal!" he said proudly, awaiting our reaction. All four of us visitors launched into immediate praise for Peter and his cooking, not just to be nice, but to salute a wonderful meal experience that we all will long remember. It really was one of the highlights of our trip, during which we trained the Czechs on leadership skills and helped them craft strategy to more effectively serve their fellow citizens and strengthen their communities. Our Champaign-Urbana team of about 12 had joined forces with the larger group of over 100 from the United States, spending a week in Prague, the capital city, before fanning out in smaller groups across the country to 10 other cities.

Though I was one of the folks doing training and teaching others during this two-week trip, I had quite the profound and powerful experience of my own. Isn't that the way it works in life? Here I was, thinking I was the one going to this country to "give away," but in the end, I was the one who ended up receiving one of my most life-changing moments ever.

Our trip had started with a flight from Chicago to Frankfurt, followed by a nine-hour bus ride to Prague. It was on the bus trip where I first realized that I wasn't in Kansas anymore. Feeling queasy from airline cuisine, the bus trip undid me. On one of our rest stops, near the Plzen brewery (famous for originating the world's first pilsner beer!), I vomited up most of what I had eaten in the previous 12 hours. Shortly thereafter, we arrived at our dormitory in Prague, a temporary stopover before being assigned to various host homes in the city. The dorm meal that night was not recognizable, at least by American standards. I could barely get any food down. I knew then and there that despite the fact that we were the teaching team, I was going to be the one learning some new life lessons on this trip.

Everything about our experiences there seemed to create discomfort and heighten my sense of vulnerability. Peter's meal notwithstanding, most of the food was strange. The toilet paper was thin and rough. Few people spoke English, with the majority speaking Czech, German, or Russian. Road signs, building signs, and restaurant menus were undecipherable (so much for my two-week language course!). The infrastructure seemed antiquated and confusing. This was indeed a country emerging from the icy grip of communism, still finding its way as it straddled centuries of history and a bold, new, postmodern world around it. Only a couple of days into our two-week visit, I began to break down.

I pulled John to the side after Peter's fabulous dinner. "John," I said, "I'm not quite sure what I'm experiencing right now, but I'm feeling incredibly uneasy. Do you have a minute?"

"Sure. You want to go outside?"

We stepped outside the apartment, shrouded in the deepening gloom of night, feeling the warm summer air waft over us. John was a man of intense faith and resolute focus, balanced, with a terrific sense of humor. I admired his authenticity and the fact that he didn't take himself too seriously.

"So, what's going on?" John asked.

"Well, it's hard to say this succinctly, but being over here has made me realize something that I'm not sure I would have realized otherwise," I said. "Basically, I just feel out of synch. Like I'm not being very effective in most of the important areas of my life."

He let that rather profound statement settle for a few moments as we listened to a bit of traffic from a nearby street, accentuated by a chorus of crickets from a grassy lot beside the apartment building.

"So are you talking work life or home life or both?"

"All that and more," I said. "I mean, work's going fine, in a way. The job's going well. But I'm feeling pretty fractured in most everything else I'm doing."

"Such as…?"

"In particular, I'm not being a very good father or husband right now, with all of the demands on my time. It just seems that I should be offering them so much more, but how do I find the time and the energy? Complicating the situation, there are so many other demands on my time in addition to my career, that I don't see much light at the end of the tunnel."

Articulating that helped me grasp the core of my uneasiness. Despite the fact that I had recently been promoted to partner in my accounting firm, had a loving wife and three children, and from all appearances seemed to be successful, I felt like a failure drowning in a sea of over-commitment. John nodded, and leaned over to touch my shoulder.

"I think I can help," he said, smiling warmly. "But it might be a little painful. Is that okay?"

"I guess so. Let's do it."

We went back inside and sat at the kitchen table while the others talked in the living room. John had me take out a sheet of paper and identify the major roles in my life, starting with the obvious—husband, father, accounting firm partner—and going on to add my roles in outside organizations, such as boards I served on and my roles in my church. I stopped when I got to eight roles, including Youth for Christ board member, neighborhood association president, church small group leader, church training school teacher, and board member for another company. Seeing it in black and white had a visceral effect on me, and I said as much to John.

"Well, we aren't done," John said. "Let's go a step deeper. Let's take your work role and break it down into major responsibilities that are core to your everyday job while also listing any 'extra assignments' you've added."

"Okay," I said. "Well, in addition to serving my clients, I am leading a team of ten. That's a pretty full plate for starters. And, I've taken on some additional local responsibilities in business development. Beyond that, I'm doing some national-scope work in coordinating business valuation services for the firm and serving on the AICPA Committee on Business Valuation Services."

Was I really doing all of this stuff? How had I managed to say yes to all of these things? While I enjoyed most of these roles, it was pretty obvious why I was feeling like a failure in the roles that mattered most.

"Have I just said yes to too many things?" My question seemed to have an obvious answer.

"That's part of it. But there is an even deeper issue here," John said.

"Like what? It seems pretty obvious to me. I've loaded up the plate with too many roles, forcing me to slice my time into too many pieces."

John looked me directly in the eye and asked me a profound and disturbing question, one I'd never been asked: "Which of these roles are in alignment with what you perceive to be your calling or core purpose in life?"

The question wasn't about too many roles per se. Nor was it about which roles I liked or which roles I was gifted in to execute. John was asking about something a level or two deeper—and that was, "Which roles really, clearly fit with my calling?"

That question, of course, begged the bigger question: "What did I understand my calling and core purpose to be?" At some level, I had wrestled with this question a few years prior, and had felt empowered coming out of the small group leader retreat in 1989. From that weekend on, I had understood my calling to be in the business world, essentially centered on my professional consulting work. But I hadn't taken it much deeper than that. I hadn't really taken the time to articulate anything more specific.

"Ok," I said. "I get the question—but I think I need to back up a bit here and answer the bigger question you've posed within the question."

"I think you're right," John said. "While I think you have a general understanding of your calling, based on what you've shared with me these last few years, I think you've got a little more work to do." John suggested I work on explaining my calling while he grabbed a second slice of cherry pie.

Over the next twenty minutes, I did my best to outline specific aspects of my calling. Yes, it had a lot to do with being a top-notch management consultant; that was my baseline. And being a leader. But it also had something to do with being a leader of leaders. It was about investing in key relationships within my "circle of influence." It had something to do with becoming totally integrated across all of my life roles. It had to do with not being satisfied with my current professional status, but nurturing a desire to become a more well-rounded practitioner of strategy and organizational high performance.

John wiped the pie crumbs from his mouth as he slid beside me at the kitchen table to check up on my progress.

"Hey, great job here, Tim. Looks you're making some headway."

"I think so," I said. "But I'm still not sure what I do with this."

"Let's examine each of your roles and see which ones fit the best with your written statements of life purpose, at this point in your life."

"Ok, but that's gonna be tough. I like pretty much all of this stuff!"

John explained that that's why so many people had difficulty in ordering their lives. They didn't closely examine which activities or pursuits fit in with achieving their life purpose. "If God has called you to something unique, and I believe he has," John said, "it most likely means that you're going to have to say no to some things. Maybe a lot of things."

And so it was with me. I had said "yes" to a lot of roles—because I enjoyed them, or had a skill that fit with the role, or because someone had asked me to do something. My plate had filled up, and indeed, it had runneth over. However, unlike David's cup in Psalm 23, it wasn't overflowing with blessings. Instead, it was overflowing with obligations and duties and responsibilities that were keeping me from my true calling. It was amazing to see it all laid out in black and white on a placemat in front of me.

I knew then that I needed to begin saying "no" to some of the roles on that piece of paper, so that I could say a louder, clearer "yes" to those roles that were in the highest degree of alignment with my core purpose. I knew that this was not going to be an overnight process; I knew it was going to take some additional thinking and praying time. And then, over the ensuing months, I would have to summon the courage to say "no" as I systematically eliminated stuff from my plate. As a people-pleaser, this was one of the toughest things I had to do—saying "no" to people and things that I enjoyed!

The remaining days on that mission trip flew by quickly, as I was energized by the interaction John and I had shared that evening. In retrospect, our interaction had an otherworldly, God-feel to it. John had, in a very skillful and caring way, led me through an exercise that would fundamentally change my life. I returned to the States with a newfound commitment to delve even more deeply into asking God to show me the specifics of my life calling and purpose.

Likewise, I asked for (and received!) a lot of grace to begin trimming roles and activities from my long list. That revelatory evening with John, over the course of the next several months, enabled me to trim back significantly on four or five of the roles on that piece of paper. In exchange for giving these things up, I had more time to devote to the remaining roles—and more energy and brainpower to contribute as well. In fact, the next two to three years proved to be one of the most pivotal periods of my life. It would be, in retrospect, the beginning of my days as a risk-taker.

PART 2

Risking it

A lot of my early life experience had to do with risk avoidance. Staying inside my comfort zone. Calculating very carefully whether a new experience would potentially prove damaging or too costly. And then in late 1994, at the peak of my career success, I was asked to consider moving to California. To start over. This was the largest risk I'd yet faced. The downside was considerable. The potential costs enormous. But there was something irresistible about the challenge.

14. Go West, Young Man!

Champaign, Illinois
November 1994

IT WAS ABOUT 5:45 P.M. ON A TUESDAY, AND I WAS EXHAUSTED. It had been a long day, and I was ending it by having a staring contest with my computer. I was hanging in there, though my eyes were glazing over.

"Hey, Tim, you okay?" Bob Harrington said as he strolled into my office. Bob was one of my brightest team members—a manager over the human resources consulting group and an expert in compensation consulting. "You look sort of…"

"Comatose?" I said, finally managing to avert my eyes from my computer. "I think I am. Too many projects. Hard to keep them all straight in my head."

"Funny thing, being in the management consulting business. It's kind of like running a restaurant," Bob said as he plopped down in a chair.

"Oh, really?" I said. "Enlighten me." I could think of a lot of things that this business was like, but a restaurant wasn't one of them.

"Think of it this way," Bob said. "Our clients are like customers at the restaurant. They've come to us with very specific expectations and needs. Of course, everyone wants something slightly different. They've placed their orders, and as far as they are concerned, they should be our top priority. Never mind that we're serving fifteen different parties at the same time. Everybody likes to think they're number one in the queue."

I shrugged and nodded. "That's probably why I'm comatose right now. Lots of demands. Tough problems to solve. And everyone wants their solution now."

Bob headed off down the hall and I shut off my computer and thought about the only problem I really wanted to solve: what's for dinner. But before I went home, I thought about the intensity of our consulting work. It demanded that we find ways to renew "on the fly," catching little respites here and there. I stood and looked out my window and across Fox Drive. I was struck by the soothing scene in front on me—a winding walking trail surrounded by trees and shrubbery, covered with a half inch of freshly fallen snow. The street and parking lot glistened with whiteness.

It was late November, 1994, and winter seemed to have arrived though the calendar indicated it was not official for another four weeks or so. Yes, I thought. Our work is really challenging and exhausting—but it's also very rewarding. We get to make a real difference for our clients, solving very challenging problems. Not only that, I get to do it with people like Bob, Tony, Kevin, Scott, Sherry, Thane and Kim—just a terrific team of talented pros. 1994 had been perhaps the most productive and fruitful year for our consulting team. We seemed to really be hitting stride.

My moment of quiet reflection was interrupted by the phone ringing. The caller ID showed an unfamiliar number, a 619 area code. I picked it up, and on the other end of the line was Pat Tabor, managing partner of our firm's San Diego office. Pat and I had been promoted to senior manager in the same class—1989. We had both attended the outdoor adventure training course in Colorado that summer, enjoying white water rafting, a challenging ropes course, and lots of good old-fashioned team building in a rugged environment. All of the newly minted senior managers bonded during that experience.

I liked Pat's ambitious style—you could certainly tell that he was going places. In short order, Pat was made a partner in the firm, then managing partner of the San Diego office. He was on the fast track, building a successful and rapidly growing practice. In fact, I had traveled recently to the San Diego office to assist on a large valuation project for a waste management firm in Tijuana. The atmosphere in the office was contagious, with about 50 pros working together with some exciting clients.

Pat wasn't just making a courtesy call that afternoon, as I quickly learned after some brief chitchat.

"Tim, let me get right to the point. Your work was top notch on that Tijuana project, and that's one of the reasons—among others—that I'd like you to consider relocating to San Diego. I'd like you to build a consulting group from scratch, right here. You've done it in Champaign—how about taking your act to a bigger stage? Are you up to the challenge?"

I let Pat's words hang in the air a minute, penetrating my psyche.

"You mean...well, like...move to...I mean, transfer to San Diego and head up a new consulting group?" I must have sounded completely confused, stammering and grasping for the right words.

"Exactly, Tim. And I'd like you to join the senior leadership team of the office and help us continue what we've started here. This is a tiger by the tail, Tim. I want you to be part of it."

I told Pat I'd call him on Thursday. I had a few dozen questions running through my mind, all of which demanded answers before giving this notion serious consideration. But the momentary shock I was experiencing derailed any coherent thoughts. Best to hang up and sort it out before saying anything too stupid.

Bam. There it was. Twenty minutes earlier, my reality had been the problems of the day, thoughts about the reward of working with the Champaign team, and a moment of quiet reflection before heading home. And, now an early Christmas present, you might say, had dropped in from the west coast. Just what was inside that package? The idea of pulling up stakes and moving Toni, Alyssa, Audra, and Kaley

2,000 miles across the country was preposterous. Surreal. Crazy. Unnerving. And yet, compelling.

I headed toward the parking lot. That didn't just happen, did it? I asked myself. Move to San Diego? And why? I'm actually quite happy here, and my consulting career is just beginning to accelerate. This doesn't even deserve twenty minutes of consideration.

I got into my car, inserted the key, listened to the hum of the engine, and reconsidered my position. OK, maybe I should give this more than twenty minutes of thought. San Diego is an amazing city. The office there is really making things happen. This could be an amazing next step for me. San Diego. I let the idea sink in a bit. The big city on a magnificent bay. Southern California. Sunshine and 70's year-round. What's not to like?

I put the car in reverse, pulled out of the parking lot, and headed home. And had second thoughts about my second thoughts. That is the most ludicrous thing I could ever do. Move to San Diego? The very definition of risking it all for the fantasy of "what might be." Just plain nuts. I love my job here in Champaign. I love my coworkers. The camaraderie we have is special. It would make no sense whatsoever to step out of this success into the unknown, essentially starting over.

I was lost in a fog of thought and the car was driving itself down Kirby Avenue. In our ten years of marriage, Toni and I had traveled to California a couple of times for pleasure, and I had been there many times for business. I'd always loved the Golden State and thought it had more than its fair share of magnificent features—mountains, redwoods, coastline, ocean, deserts, and of course, Disneyland. I envied the lucky folks who got to call Southern California home. But moving a family of three daughters and spouse to live there? That was a different matter entirely.

Pulling into the driveway, I recalled a conversation that Toni and I had about one year prior. We were visiting San Diego for a meeting of the American Institute of CPA's Committee on Business Valuation, staying at the magnificent Hotel Del Coronado. Strolling down the sidewalk on our way back from dinner one night, we were nearly knocked over by a towheaded, long-haired "typical" California teenager whizzing in front of us on a skateboard.

"Sheesh. Watch out, buddy!" the teen yelled.

"Hey, you're the one on the skateboard on a sidewalk," I helpfully reminded him. "You watch out!"

"Could you imagine raising kids here?" I asked Toni, categorically grouping all California youths into my tidy mental box, constructed with Midwestern-inspired wisdom.

"Are you serious? This is a different world altogether," she replied. "No way."

That pretty much summed things up.

So as I turned off the engine, got out of the car, and pressed the garage door button, I pretty well knew what to expect when I dropped the bomb on Toni in about two minutes.

"You're never going to believe what just happened, honey," I announced.

"Do you want water or lemonade with the pork chops tonight?" Toni was placing ice in the dinner glasses. The kids were upstairs in the play room.

"Water's fine."

"Alright, then. Have a seat. Now, what's the big news?"

I related the details about the call from Pat Tabor, the offer to move to San Diego and head up a new consulting team there, and that Pat and I would be talking again in a couple of days. Toni listened intently, a glint in her eye.

"I know this is all very strange, pretty much unrealistic, and otherwise crazy," I said. "So, I can just tell him 'thanks but no thanks' and let it end there."

Toni looked me directly in the eye, gently put her left hand on top of my right, and calmly said, "I think we should consider this."

And so, for most of December, we pondered and prayed and discussed the possibility of moving west. And felt exhilarated. And sad. And joyful. And empowered with a sense of new freedom. We also felt the bottom of our stomachs drop out a few times, as if we were on the

Screamin' Eagle Roller Coaster ride. We quietly (and selectively) shared the opportunity with a few family members and close friends. While all of them seemed excited, few could see us really going through with such a major move. That was a bit dispiriting. In retrospect, I've learned that cross-country moves are difficult on everyone—but they seem to have a disproportionate impact on those we leave behind. The sense of loss is more "present" on a daily basis, while the party that moves away seems to be distracted with all of the new adventure.

Toni and I visited San Diego the week after Christmas and naturally it rained most of the week, with unseasonably chilly weather to boot. Figures. We met the San Diego partner team and their spouses during a lovely dinner at Mister A's, overlooking the twinkling lights of downtown San Diego and its harbor, with a front row seat to the flight path of all aircraft landing at Lindbergh Field. We toured neighborhoods and schools. We hit North County, East County, Coastal, Downtown, and Inland. We visited shopping centers and beaches. And, we talked to many of the folks in the office—only three of whom were native San Diegans, the rest being transplants from other parts of the country. We sat at the (cloudy) pool and wondered out loud about the ridiculousness of such a big move. We laughed and we cried, and at the end of the week the process was, if nothing else, a great exercise in strengthening our marital communication!

When we returned home, we continued the process of talking with close friends, counseling with our pastors and parents, and praying quietly with one another for emerging direction. Interestingly, I've often thought that major life decisions should be carefully weighed over a period of time—and that one should seek out multiple confirmations when a major change appears imminent. This is not entirely unlike listing pros and cons of a decision and seeing which side of the ledger weighs more—but it goes well beyond that. It consists of really opening ourselves up to seek the confluence of three things—God's leading, friendly and unbiased counsel from those we trust, and a settled "knowing" deep within our spirit. When these three align and confirm one another, then the right answer often emerges.

And indeed, as January unfolded, Toni and I began to sense an emerging clarity. Scripture verses and sermons spoke to us about taking risks and trusting God. Our closest friends began to reluctantly affirm that the move seemed to be the right thing to do, though they couldn't quite explain it. In my quiet time, a profound sense of wonderment would come over me as I envisioned our family living in the San Diego suburbs. Vivid dreams about the possibilities began to take root in me, and my spirit became dislodged from its familiar routines and comfort zone. In my mind's eye, and with considerable delight, I pictured Toni and myself leaping from the cliff's edge into the deep, blue water below.

By the end of the month our minds (and spirits) were made up. We would indeed accept the offer and move west. It didn't seem completely rational—and, in fact, I could make stronger logical arguments against the move than for it. But Toni and I were jointly swept up in a powerful eddy of God's direction, the embrace of our closest friends and counselors, and an unshakeable conviction in our spirits that the move was our destiny. Mindful, of course, of the move's impact on our three children (10, 7, and 4 at the time), we brought them into an understanding of our decision as best we could.

The energy and excitement surrounding the move made it no less difficult to contemplate our departure, leaving behind all of our extended family, saying goodbye to a great work team, and turning my back on what was surely a solid opportunity to continue building the consulting practice in Champaign. The "saying goodbye" process, fortunately, occurred over several months' time—from January through May. And over that time, we were able to contemplate and make plans for building a life in our soon-to-be new neighborhood, new school, new office, with new friends… and a new way of life. I was able to make several trips to San Diego to begin the transition process and lay the foundation for building a new consulting team. Toni and the girls were able to visit over spring break, to get a handle on what life as Californians would be like, and see the home site we purchased in a new tract development in Rancho de los Penasquitos.

As moving day approached, the gravity of what we were doing did indeed sink in. This was a major life change—and one that would impact all of us, for the balance of our lives. That sobering realization made Toni and me stop and reconfirm our decision more than once. Inflection points are often this way—two great choices, one perhaps more familiar and one inherent with both risk and new opportunity. But reconfirm our choice we did, and on May 29, 1995, with the moving van fully packed and already on its way, we loaded up the Dodge Grand Caravan and hit Interstate 57 South. We had some fun stops along the way—Grand Canyon, Petrified Forest, a gold mine, and a ghost town, to name a few. The trip was actually quite delightful. Pulling into our temporary apartment home at La Mirage Apartments on the evening of June 1, we collapsed into bed that night, exhausted. Funny thing, we awoke the morning of June 2, our 11th anniversary and first without exchanging cards or gifts—somehow in the hustle and bustle of the move, we'd both lost track of an otherwise important celebration. We both burst out laughing at that, kissed each other, and Toni said to me, "Happy anniversary, dear. Thanks for taking me on this awesome adventure. And by the way, welcome to our new life!"

15. Teamwork

San Diego, California
April 1995

"TIM, YOU'RE LOOKING PRETTY GASSED RIGHT NOW,"
Ken Ritzman said as I jogged by him, huffing and puffing, on my way back to my cabin. Ken was the lead tax partner in the San Diego office.

"Wow, Ken," I panted, stopping a moment and putting my hands on my knees. "We don't have terrain like this" (huff, huff) "back in Illinois. That was a pretty challenging run."

"Enjoy it in, my friend. We have mountains, beaches, sunshine, and plenty of other new experiences for you here in San Diego," Ken laughed.

The run that morning on winding mountain pathways had been one of the more challenging sessions of exercise I'd ever been through. Twenty minutes in, and I knew I wasn't in Illinois anymore. The Whispering Winds Catholic Retreat center, nestled rustically in the northern part of San Diego County near Julian, was an absolutely beautiful setting. The dorm-like accommodations were spare, but the natural beauty more than made up for that.

I had joined my future work colleagues on their annual all-office retreat in April, 1995, about two months before my family and I would be moving to San Diego. I'd heard about the retreat during my recruitment to the San Diego office. Several folks had mentioned that it was a highlight for them, and that they eagerly looked forward to it. Rather unique in accounting firm culture, the retreat was an opportunity for the entire office staff to go off-line together for two days (after tax season, of course!). Everyone—secretaries, first-year staff auditors, senior-level partners, managers, and all in-between—was invited to share meals together, engage in meaningful conversation regarding the most pressing issues facing the company, spend some free time reflecting, and go through a pretty novel set of team problem-solving exercises that redefined what it meant to "work together."

As I cooled down, the pungent smell of pine trees was a welcome relaxer. The early-morning air was crisp—in fact, I could see my breath. I had about 30 minutes to shower and make my way down to the main meeting hall where we would officially start the day with a hearty breakfast, prepared by the office crew assigned for that morning's meal (no fancy catering here). Following that, we were broken down into teams of seven and briefed on the main exercise for the day—a scavenger hunt where we would decipher clever clues while crisscrossing the retreat grounds for few hours. The hunt would then transition to an exercise to create a "nature collage" representing our team's view of the company's future.

Pat Tabor, the managing partner of the office, also gave us a preview of the next day's activities—specifically mentioning the Alligator Pit, Dead Man's Crossing, and Rest in Peace exercises. He seemed to take particular delight in watching our reactions as he read off a description of each "game." The competitive ones in the group let out whoops and hollers, while some in the group noticeably groaned, and others looked pensive. It was all part of the design—getting us out of our comfort zones and the familiar surroundings of the office.

Though I didn't fully realize it at the time, the retreat experience was a microcosm of the next several years in San Diego. From that point forward, I would gain a new appreciation for nature and God's incredible variety of creation. I would work with others in ways I'd not previously experienced—solving tough challenges very much as a team—and seeing the fruit of success as a result. I would experience a deeper integration of my personal sense of purpose with a larger purpose—that of the company's, but more importantly, that of the Creator's. I would be immersed into a corporate culture that valued people, challenged them, and rewarded them. In this regard, and perhaps most importantly, the leadership of the San Diego McGladrey office was reflecting the image of the Creator by the manner in which they designed the office to function.

As I drove to the hotel on Saturday evening following the conclusion of the retreat, God's Spirit spoke to me: "Tim, the leaders of this office may not fully realize it, but they have created a catalytic environment that is aligned with my purposes. I've brought you here to add to the mix, but I've been way out of ahead of you on this. Get ready for an amazing ride."

While on one hand I was excited and pumped, I was also confused.

"Lord," I asked, "How could the leadership have done this, with none of them professing Christians? Don't we have to consciously choose to cooperate with you?"

I didn't hear an answer to my question. Alone in silence, I pondered the question and the deep ramifications of it. Do humans need to choose to align with God in order for him to use them? I'd always assumed so. Certainly, it makes it easier for God to accomplish what he wants, I surmised. But then again, perhaps I had restricted God in my own mind—limited him, maybe. Another twenty minutes of driving, and I was pretty sure I'd put God in my Tim-defined box, and he was showing me that he wasn't going to be confined there. Furthermore, he was serving me notice that the next four years were going to be a time of significant paradigm shifts for me.

I pulled the car into the parking lot of the hotel that evening, pausing before proceeding to the lobby. I bowed my head in quiet prayer. "Lord, I give you permission to completely remove any restrictions I've placed on you. Show me how big you are. Help me to cooperate with your most awesome plan. Amen."

A revolution had begun. My spirit was ablaze. I was ready to immerse myself in this new milieu, joining Pat Tabor and Ken Ritzman as the newest member of the senior leadership team of the San Diego office.

Pat, lead partner in the audit practice, was also the partner-in-charge of the office. Ken was the lead partner over the tax practice. I joined as the leader of the consulting practice unit. While the three of us comprised the senior leadership team of the office, other partners included Patricia Sbarbaro, Joe LaPlante, Rory Gordon, Steve Austin, and Grant Brisacher.

The "young thinking," entrepreneurial environment created by Pat and Ken, along with the other partners in the San Diego office, was incredibly attractive and emotionally healthy. This was an office committed to excellence and one that was in a mode of continuous learning and improvement. The San Diego office embodied a philosophy of "who before what." They were careful to make hires of great talent because they understood the fundamental business principle that great people make great companies. After moving there, I knew that this principle would be essential in establishing a top-performing consulting group, something the office had not had in prior years. Toward that end, I courted and convinced two of my key team members in the consulting group from Illinois—Tony Moore and Bob Harrington—to relocate to San Diego and join me in building a first-rate team. Both were top-notch consultants, and each liked what he saw happening in the San Diego office. It really didn't take too much convincing, now that I think back on it.

In many ways, the leadership of the office embraced a dynamic of serving employees while simultaneously serving customers. These elements really do go together, but so many companies don't seem to understand the vital link between the two. The office was actively creating a catalytic environment with employees given challenging work, afforded ample opportunity for advancement, and being personally rewarded for their individual contribution to the overall effort. As our office prospered, we shared that prosperity with the people making it happen, in both monetary and nominal ways. Our goal was for each person to be compensated at a "market or above" salary, with opportunities for performance bonuses.

Beyond the important cash compensation, there were a variety of other "forms of payment" in this employee-focused culture. A few examples: a "snack room" offered a plethora of fruit, bagels, drinks and snacks, completely free of charge, along with complimentary meals routinely brought into the office during peak seasons. Employees were offered flexible schedules to tend to personal and family matters. As long as the assigned work was completed, employees were free to schedule their personal and work time accordingly. A "fun committee" planned and organized events like the annual "day at the Del Mar horse races," Christmas parties, and summer picnics. Employees routinely enjoyed Padres baseball games and Chargers football games with clients and prospective clients of the firm, not to mention our families.

The importance of a vibrant workplace environment has proven vital for the employees of many companies. The most current research has found that the environment in which people work can make a dramatic impact on their motivation, commitment to the company, and their overall sense of well-being. Indeed, companies that make a proactive effort to create a stimulating, creative, and supportive environment will see the return on investment in spades. Yet, many companies are still figuring this out. In this regard, I consider myself fortunate to have been part of an organization committed to creating and maintaining a culture of excellence with a focus on its employees—well before much of the present-day research indicated this is what they should do. The San Diego office of McGladrey afforded me the privilege of experiencing first hand a "Thank God It's Monday!" corporate culture for over three years. Keenly aware of the unique things happening in my workplace, I began to develop a real desire to share the story with others. How much fun would it be to encourage people that it is possible to experience fulfillment in one's work? Too much, I decided—and that's when I began to actively explore the idea of writing a book.

16. Thank God It's Monday!

Los Angeles, California
September 1997

THE TRAIN AMBLED ITS WAY UP THE PACIFIC COAST, rocking side to side, the early morning sun reflecting off the ocean to my left. I was surrounded by the rugged, beautiful, and largely undeveloped expanse known as Camp Pendleton, a Marine Corps base. Sandwiched between the sprawling urban development of San Diego and Orange County, this anomaly remains the largest undeveloped portion of Southern California coastline. The ecosystem is diverse—with beaches to the west and mountains to the east—and bluffs, mesas, canyons, and a river in between. It was a lovely way to begin what would be a life-altering meeting with a professional literary agent in Los Angeles, Ken Atchity of AEI. Ken and I had been corresponding via phone and email for a couple of months about a book writing project, but this would be our first face-to-face meeting.

"Do you see the dolphins out there?" an older woman seated behind me exclaimed.

Most of us in the rail car momentarily diverted our attention from our newspapers, books, and laptops to look left. Sure enough, a pod of four dolphins seemed to be racing us up the coast. They were leaping out of the water in what appeared to be a synchronized dance.

"Wow. Cool!" A 10-year-old boy in a Dodgers' ball cap added. "Are those the ones from Sea World, Mom?"

"No honey, those are dolphins in the wild."

Very cool indeed. Dolphins in the wild. Swimming side by side and leaping into the air. Their graceful movements elicited a smile in my spirit. In fact, they reflected perfectly the deep, inner emotions I was experiencing that morning. Emotions of profound joy and excitement about the new opportunity that was about to unfold in another hour or so.

Other than the risky step of moving to California, I had pretty much followed a conventional path up to that point in life. Do well in high school, get a college degree in a marketable discipline (accounting), join a respectable firm and climb the ladder to partner. Build a consulting team in Champaign, Illinois, and then transfer to the San Diego office to tackle the bigger challenge of building a team in a large market. The move to California had certainly been full of challenges—but they were manageable within the bounds of a firm and industry that I understood pretty well. The step I would take that particular day was one into completely alien territory. I would soon be opening the door to writing a book. The opportunity was inviting and seemed innocent enough. I'd just add the project of writing a book to my already reasonably full to-do list of projects. Simple enough.

Over the course of my collegiate years and early professional career, I had the idea that I wanted to write a book someday. Most of my thoughts along these lines were fleeting, easy to put off until another day. I had a mortgage to pay and a family to care for—and a full-time job that demanded more than its fair share of energy and attention. But the thoughts continued to recur—and they grew more real in the mid-'90s when I relocated to San Diego. Something about Southern California, with its possibility thinking, stirred me regularly and clarified my vision for writing.

I had thoughts of book themes on more personal topics, and other times thoughts of a work-related concepts and ideas. My experiences with my consulting team in Champaign, taken to even greater depths of enjoyment in San Diego, ultimately helped me crystallize a vision for a book around the concept of a "toolkit" of resources that could assist people in discovering and aligning their life purpose and their work (a topic, by the way, that you will notice I am still working on!). Little did I know, the creation of this book would set off an interesting string of events that would cause me to rethink and refocus my entire career.

As I stepped off the train at Union Station in LA, looking for Ken Atchity, I thought of what he had said to me after we had gone back and forth about the book: "Why don't we get together and see if we can do a deal?" Words every aspiring author longs to hear.

Ken waved to me, and I walked over to him, smiling. We shook hands. He had the appearance of a kindly grandfather, salt and pepper hair, a few visible wrinkles on the forehead and a bit of a twinkle in his eye.

"So what do you think of Union Station, Tim?" Ken asked.

"Beautiful. I've seen it in a movie or two—but it's more impressive in person."

"Yes, it is. In fact, they're shooting something over in the corner there as we speak," Ken said.

Sure enough, directly in front of us, a crew of eight looked to be shooting a television commercial or something of that sort. I experienced a small adrenaline rush. This was definitely a different world, I said to myself.

As we sat down for lunch at a café about a block down the street, Ken asked me why I wanted to write a book.

"I suppose you hear a lot of people say, 'I've always wanted to write a book,' so I won't use that line," I said.

He waited patiently for me to find the words.

"I guess I want to convey a message that I am passionate about," I said. "That is, discovering and exploring a sense of personal purpose and then figuring out how to align that with the right kind of work and workplace. I think I've learned some things about that process, having gone through it firsthand—and a book seems the perfect way to share that experience with the world."

"Good answer," Ken said, giving me a wrinkled smile. "Writing a book is a bit like birthing a baby—or at least that's what the females in my office tell me. You are pregnant with an idea, a concept. Something that really grips you, something that resonates deeply. And in the fullness of time, you have to give birth. You bring expression to your idea by writing."

"That's exactly how I feel," I said excitedly. I was beaming from ear to ear, unable to throttle the emotion I was experiencing. Inside I was saying I am ready to do this! I am ready to share this powerful message with the world—and I need your help, Ken! Somehow, he picked up on all that.

"Yes, I can sense that you're ready. As we've talked over the last few months, I've become increasingly intrigued with your book topic. But I felt it was important to meet you and get a better sense of why you're so interested in this project. I'm going to take you on as a client, Tim. You're not my typical client, mind you, but I like you. I think you have a compelling message and you seem ready to work hard to develop it."

True enough. And so Ken Atchity, who normally worked with higher profile clients on Hollywood projects, offered me a literary representation contract. Over tuna tartare and minestrone soup, we proceeded to work out a detailed task list and project timetable.

On the train ride back to San Diego, again amidst some of the most stunning natural beauty on earth, I recall experiencing a wide range of emotions that could most appropriately be described as euphoria. This was a dream and a vision coming true—the opportunity to put into print some exciting ideas that I strongly believed in and to become a published author. While I had envisioned writing a book for years, the fact that it was now becoming a reality was somewhat overwhelming.

As a first order of business, Ken had assigned one of his freelance editors, John Shapiro, to work with me on the project. I scheduled a session with John in Newport Beach to begin working through a long list of stuff—style of writing, target audience, the essence of the content I would produce, timing on producing the work, how we would work together, etc. In that first meeting, we decided the book would be titled Thank God It's Monday! with the subtitle A Toolkit for Aligning Your Lifevision with Your Work. The basic premise was to offer a set of practical guidelines for discovering and fleshing out one's purpose and then finding a way to align that purpose with one's work. I personally liked the TGIM acronym, because I strongly believed that people whose interests were truly aligned with their purpose would be eager to go to work on Mondays, instead of just "getting through" the work week, waiting for Friday to arrive.

After this initial excitement wore off, it was time to get to work. To get the book into the upcoming spring season, we decided on a compressed time frame of three months to write the book, edit it, and prepare it for publication. We also had to prepare a book proposal to sell it to a publisher. Together, John, Ken, and I went to work. I wrote most of the book at the Mission Trails Regional Park library, about eight miles northeast of downtown San Diego. It was an inspiring setting, with the San Diego River running through Mission Gorge, Fortuna Mountain Saddle and Cowles Mountain framing the perimeter of the park, and the Old Mission Dam offering a powerful history lesson dating over 200 years.

I would typically take a half-day or full day per workweek to camp out in the library and write. Meanwhile, I was required to keep up my full-time commitment as a consulting partner with McGladrey & Pullen. Our work team had very specific "chargeable hour" goals—and I certainly wasn't going to be let off the hook from those while writing. That meant more work on evenings and weekends. But the sacrifice was worth it. Writing, and looking forward to the finished product, energized me—and that extra energy became the fuel for getting my other work done.

Not only was I experiencing previously untapped energy for my day-to-day work, but the writing and reflecting process began to produce a shift in my thinking regarding my career and sense of calling. At first, the shift was subtle—and then it became more obvious. One of obvious objectives for the book was engaging each reader to plumb the depths of his or her purpose. Funny thing, but the more I read and reread drafts of each chapter, the more I felt the words speaking back to me. It dawned on me that I had only a theoretical understanding of what I was writing. As time went on, it became clearer and clearer to me: It was time to practice what I was preaching to my readers. I had assumed I would be challenging my readers; I found I was really challenging myself.

For fifteen years, I had enjoyed the "friendly confines" of a professional services firm—one that provided stimulating work, terrific peers, plentiful resources, and financial prosperity. It's time to do something different, I began to hear over and over. Time to get better aligned. Time to make a significant change. Time to take a risk.

I took a mental and emotional inventory. What did it mean to get better aligned? Just how risky would that be and what would it consist of? Was I really ready to make a major change in my career? How would this impact my family? Was it really time to take a big step into the unknown? The questions were numerous. The answers, inconclusive. The process, emotionally wrenching.

I suppose in one way, the prospect of making a substantial change to become better aligned was thrilling—but in a more practical and rational way, it was quite terrifying. For several weeks, I experienced a tug-of-war between the emerging sense of the "new and exciting" with the "solid and familiar." This was not an entirely foreign conundrum to me. It seemed an awful lot like the decision process a few years prior where Toni and I wrestled with the move from comfortable, positive and "known commodity" of Illinois to the risky, tantalizing and essentially unknown California. And here I was again, contemplating a similar idea—but much sooner than I had anticipated.

"Really, God? Is this you I'm hearing?" I remember asking myself.

No answer.

"I mean, haven't I already taken a big enough risk in leaving friends, family, and career in Champaign to move to San Diego? Why ask me to take another big step so soon?" I asked, out loud.

Silence.

"The stakes are even bigger with this one, Lord. At least with the move in 1995, I had a secure job, a clear pathway. I don't know what's on the other side of this decision."

Nothing.

But unmistakably, week upon week throughout the early months of 1998, I continued to have the sense that change was imminent, that better alignment was soon to come, that risk was becoming my best friend. This whole development was really quite a surprise. Before writing the drafts of the book, I considered myself in pretty high alignment with my work—but the more I wrote, the more I had a sense that there was something exciting, adventurous, and altogether different awaiting me in the near future.

My first attempt to access this risky, alternative future was to stay within the firm but rework my focus. In April, I proposed to my fellow partners Pat and Ken that I would pursue professional speaking and workshop facilitation engagements tied back to the TGIM book, all while leading my team of consultants in their work. Pat and Ken were somewhat open to this idea, but those higher up in the firm were not buying it. That idea was ultimately rejected. What the firm needed was for me to "stick to my knitting," not pursue some fanciful notion of celebrity speaker and facilitator. By June, I found myself negotiating an amicable departure, while simultaneously making plans to form a new consulting, speaking, and training entity. As June, July, and August unfolded, the palpable sense of adventure was growing inside me. Like dozens of clients I had served over my career, I would soon be a full-fledged entrepreneur, the owner and operator of LifeVision, Inc.

I was joined in the LifeVision endeavor by a good friend and mentor, John Chisholm. John had worked as a sales professional, then pastor, and had over the '90s remade himself into a highly effective consultant in the fields of conflict resolution, team training, and strategy. He had been instrumental in helping me evaluate my life purpose (see Chapter 13), setting a series of things in motion back in 1992 that had led pretty pointedly to the writing of the book and now the leap to start this new company.

The partnership with John was a great fit; his emphasis was on soft skills (communication, leadership, and organization development) and mine was on hard skills (financial analysis, systems, organization structure, deal doing, and the like). John was based in Illinois, and for the first year, I remained in San Diego. At the time of our launch, I remember thinking I've never in my life been more excited, more prepared, more ready to take on this new thing called LifeVision! The world was indeed our oyster. So, without looking back, I took the plunge… not knowing that the plunge would soon be a freefall down the sheer face of a cliff!

17. A Setup for Success? Not.

San Diego, California
February 1999

I HAD JUST HUNG UP THE PHONE. The words were echoing in my brain cavity: "We appreciate your proposal, Tim, but we have decided not to move forward at this time. If we happen to change our minds…."

I glanced around my office. Everything seemed to have a dull, uninteresting look—the neat piles of paper, the artwork hung on the wall, coffee cup, mementos of past projects, even the jelly bean jar. The routine had become all too familiar, and I found the trend to be unnerving. That particular conversation had been just the latest potential client project to fall through. Everything seemed to be on track, only to go off the rails at the last minute—with no reasonable explanation.

I sighed and muttered "Really? Come on, Lord. If this wasn't my livelihood at stake, it would be a comedy."

Ken Gerard, an attorney just down the hall in our shared office space in the San Diego suburb of Rancho Bernardo, happened to be walking by my open door. He stuck his head in, displaying his typical big, toothy grin.

"Did you say something to me, Tim?"

"Oh, sorry, Ken—just me talking to myself, I guess."

I must have looked exactly like I was feeling inside. Ken furrowed his brow and said, "Is something wrong, my friend? You don't look well."

"Oh, it's nothing, really. Just another day at the office."

Ken wasn't buying it. "You're usually pretty upbeat, Tim, but it looks like something pretty heavy is weighing on you. What's up?"

"Just got off the phone. Another promising project down the drain," I said. "Gonna have to figure out some way to pay the bills. And, on top of that, just this week I discovered that a former colleague of mine at the firm has been strongly opposed to McGladrey sending me client referrals; he is insisting that he can do these projects. What I thought would be a nice pipeline of work has become barely a trickle."

Ken told me he'd seen dozens of business folks go through seasons of challenge, particularly when starting a business. The important thing, he said, was how I would respond. Could I embrace the negatives as a learning moment?

A strange concept. I didn't want to embrace the negatives. I wanted to eradicate them. But Ken was telling me the only way to eradicate them was to embrace them. This was not exactly starting out as I had hoped.

It wasn't just that my former colleague Larry (not his real name), was making things difficult for me and my new firm, LifeVision. Or that I was seeing potential projects go awry before they began. Or that I would soon be scrambling to find creative ways to make ends meet. The most troubling aspect of this increasingly disappointing situation was the profound sense of irony and incongruity that I was feeling. In starting LifeVision, I had never felt more prepared and more passionate about anything in my professional career. The charter of LifeVision was in full alignment with my gifting and personal vision, or so I had thought. I had believed that the prior 15 years of professional experience, and in some respects, my entire life had led up to this momentous time. And at that point, sharing with Ken my frustration, it seemed that nothing had gone as expected.

I never could have envisioned in August, 1998, what would unfold over the next 22 months—essentially one failure after another. In fact, I experienced more instances of failure in that short time than I had in the previous 36 years combined. As a result, everything I had known or assumed to be true about God was being challenged. Did he really care that I was failing so miserably? Had he "set me up" for this, knowing all along I'd fall on my face? Was he really "for me" as Pastor Bill Jackson had told me at coffee one morning? Nothing was making sense, and as the weeks progressed, it felt as if every square inch of the foundation underneath me was slowly eroding, shaking, crumbling. After having felt so well prepared, so fired up, and completely convinced that God had commissioned me to go for it, I had been reduced to questioning every aspect of my life, even unsure of my soundness of mind.

The problems started from the very beginning of the business launch in mid 1998. Larry, my former coworker, had always been a friend, supporter, and confidant of mine in the years we worked together. Somehow, my departure and resulting change in my relationship with the firm became a huge threat to him. Prior to leaving McGladrey & Pullen, I had worked out an arrangement to provide consulting services to several accounting firms that were part of the McGladrey Network. These firms were independently owned and autonomous from McGladrey, but subscribed to the Network in order to access training materials, expert resources, consulting assistance, and the like. After leaving McGladrey, Larry made it very difficult for me to continue my work with firms in the Network. While I had planned on roughly a third of our firm's revenue coming from the Network, the actual figure ended up being closer to 5%. What was supposed to be $100,000 of work turned out to be less than $20,000.

My professional identify had always been "management consultant," dating back to 1983 when I joined McGladrey as a wet-behind-the-ears graduate from Illinois State. So it was difficult to experience so many consulting project letdowns as I transitioned to a small, independent consulting practice. One instance in particular is seared in my memory. The prospect of a huge project had come up for a client in the southeast United States, and I prepared a detailed proposal for strategic planning services for this multi-location accounting firm.

There had been extensive conversation about the possible project, and I'd prepared what I thought was a winning proposal—a very client-focused, customized approach to helping them through this complex planning process. In fact, listening carefully to clients telling me their needs and crafting proposals was something I'd become quite skilled at over the years. After hearing the firm's managing director tell me this was a "sure deal," the deal surely fell apart. To add further insult, there was no explanation forthcoming and no follow-up communication. I was just left hanging.

On another occasion, I facilitated a leadership retreat for a company in Montana that went about as poorly as any project I had ever done. I remember preparing extensively for the project, interviewing several of the firm's partners in advance. Based on those interviews and the information I'd obtained, I put together an engagement approach that looked great on paper. Again, this was something I'd done successfully many times over in my career at McGladrey, and I felt good about this project. As my commuter flight approached the landing on a Thursday afternoon, I can remember surveying the surrounding beauty of the mountains and feeling energized and pumped up. I was ready to go!

But as the retreat unfolded, issue after issue surfaced that I had not anticipated. There was deep disagreement among the partners about the future direction of the company, and it also came to light that various partners didn't get along with one another. These types of fundamental problems make a team-building retreat almost impossible to pull off. A really effective team-building retreat assumes some basic level of trust and health is in place to start, and that was far from the case here.

And so, the team-building retreat ended up being akin to a Survivor episode with various factions competing against—and yelling at—each other. What had started out so promising, with partners nodding in agreement to the retreat agenda, quickly deteriorated into a perfect storm of consulting disaster. The issues that had surfaced at the retreat should have been identified in the interviews I had done several weeks prior. But, alas, either I had not asked the right questions, or there had been an inability for the partners to trust me with the sensitive nature of the information—or maybe they were fearful or too embarrassed to reveal the real issues going on in their firm. Not only did the retreat fail to get folks on the same page regarding their firm's future, but in some ways, it exacerbated tensions and made things worse. Just like the TV show, I was voted off the island.

In addition to consulting projects, one of the key pieces of my plan for revenue in LifeVision was booking professional speaking engagements. I had done all the necessary preparation work to get this portion of the business off the ground: I hired a videographer to video several of my speaking engagements and assemble a demo tape. I hired a speaker's bureau to represent me. I spent marketing dollars to create promo materials and sent dozens of promo kits to potential customers. I purchased a professional speaker's audiotape training system to perfect my craft (at considerable expense, I might add). And in 22 months, I had booked three paid speaking engagements! So much for that idea.

Other discouraging, disheartening events happened in rapid succession during those 22 months. After one unpaid speaking engagement at a service organization in Lake Forest, California, I received an anonymous, intensely threatening phone call telling me in very heated language to "take my **** philosophy and get the **** out of town." I'd spoken to that group on the basics of creating a Thank God It's Monday! corporate culture—hardly something controversial, or so I thought. Well, at least I didn't have to worry about getting out of Lake Forest, as I didn't live there to begin with. Humor aside, I remember my body shaking for a good 10 minutes after getting that phone call. How many professional speakers have audience members track them down and cuss them out? For me, it was a first, and an unsettling one at that.

Book sales were another key element of LifeVision's intended business model. The idea was to secure a speaking engagement, give the talk, and promote the book for purchase. With my great success at securing speaking gigs, this particular strategy was pretty well doomed from the start. And, unfortunately, my book publisher went bankrupt at the end of 1998, stiffing the book publicist for thousands in fees and leaving me with no real marketing chutzpah. By the end of 1999, the book had sold a few thousand copies and that was that. Another bust.

During this time, my personal journal was full of entries that screamed frustration. One such entry sums it up well:

I feel the weight of owing my investors [in LifeVision, Inc.] better than this. I feel the weight of not pulling my weight in this business venture. I feel, most of all, the weight of not doing what I feel gifted and called to do—speak, write, and creatively develop (and be able to make a living at it).

All of this has caused me serious doubts about my abilities. Is this all just a big test for me to pass? I am emotionally drained and spiritually teetering on the edge.

Maybe this is a huge wake-up call to live in reality. Quit dreaming. Quit visioning and start doing something more realistic.

Well, exasperated as I was, I didn't entirely quit dreaming and visioning. Through all of the failures, I tried to remain resilient. I kept getting back on my feet, only to be knocked down the next week. It was the darkest period of my life. I soldiered on, believing that I was indeed fulfilling my life purpose—to help people and companies develop high-performance habits while pursuing excellence.

But the frustration had taken taking a huge emotional toll. In December of 1999, I called my brother Ben (a pastor) and told him I was teetering on the edge of a decision to hang it up, and that it was becoming excruciating to go into work each day. In fact, I was having serious thoughts of doing something entirely different—like buying a truck, wheelbarrow, and some basic tools, dusting off my childhood-acquired gardening skills, and becoming a landscaper. The simplicity of that plan had, at least momentarily, a tremendous amount of appeal given the complete frustration I was experiencing as a business consultant, speaker, and author.

Always being one able to speak meaningfully into my life, Ben talked me back from the edge of the cliff and told me that he believed I was called to the business world, my present failures notwithstanding. He reaffirmed my gifts and calling, told me that God had not abandoned me, and then encouraged me to think practically and reasonably about changes I could make going forward. Perhaps LifeVision, Inc. had run its course, he said, but there were certainly other business opportunities that I should investigate. It wasn't time to "hang it up" with the business world, Ben said. Yes, I'd taken a big risk leaving the accounting firm and all of the trappings that supported me. Yes, I'd pretty much fallen flat on my face. And yes, reminiscent of the Sunday school picnic attempt to walk on the water, I was soaking wet and covered with mud. But—and it was a big but—God was far from finished with me. He was intimately acquainted with my mess—and he was still very much in love with me and "for me."

Indeed, five months later, in May 2000, the nearly two years of full-time "LifeVision, Inc. experiment" concluded with me taking a near-full-time position as president with one of my clients, SourceGear. So, while I was pretty much wrapping things up at LifeVision, Inc., I wasn't leaving the professional business world to become a landscaper. Landing that job was a great emotional relief. After the litany of rejections I had experienced in two years, the SourceGear position made me feel wanted. And, importantly, I was able to regain a sense of personal significance, something that had been almost entirely wiped out over the previous two years.

I had been taken to the end of myself. Every fiber of my faith in a Supreme Being who absolutely loves us, is intimately acquainted with our woes, and is "for us," was put to the test. And although the stripping away of my sense of self-worth had its benefits, causing me to push toward the outer boundaries of my relationship with God, I don't think he designed us to live in that state for very long. Indeed, I was profoundly grateful to emerge on the other side of those two years with a resolve to better understand my own "story" and sense of purpose, and better understand how they fit into God's bigger story.

18. In the Rearview Mirror

San Diego, California
June 1999

IT WAS ABOUT 5:15 P.M. ON MONDAY, JUNE 28, 1999. Audra (middle daughter), Sadie (golden retriever), and I were heading south on "the 15." In about 10 minutes, we would be connecting with "the 8," heading east toward Illinois, leaving San Diego in the rearview mirror. Earlier that day we had taken Toni, Alyssa, and Kaley to the airport for their flight. Audra and I got assigned the unenviable task of road-tripping with the family dog for the ensuing 36 hours (the first 12 of which Sadie refused to sit down).

The tears began to flow as we listened to soft worship music. This was my last trip down the 15 as a resident of San Diego, a trip I'd taken hundreds of times before. The sense of loss was tangible, real. Almost overwhelming. The uncertainty of our new future weighed on my heart, creating a physical sensation of pain. What had been the most energizing chapter in our lives—the previous four years in San Diego—had come to an end. And it was not the end I had envisioned.

"Why are you crying, Dad?"

"It's... it's hard to say goodbye, Audi," I sniffed.

"But we already said goodbye to the neighbors this morning," she chirped, looking at me quizzically.

You gotta love the perspective of an eleven-year-old.

"What I mean is, it's hard to say goodbye to a wonderful place where we've lived for four years and built solid relationships. A place where a big vision and exciting new things came to life –and then changed abruptly. So now, we are turning the page to a new chapter…" I choked back tears as my voice trailed off.

Audra hesitated, and I could tell her brain gears were cranking. I was concerned about displaying such raw emotion openly, but I lacked the resolve to hold it in.

"We'll be okay, right?" Audra asked.

"Oh, yeah, we'll be okay, Audi." I smiled slightly.

"God's in control, right?"

"Yes, he is. Sometimes it doesn't look like it, but he is. We've got to trust him as this new chapter unfolds. We're saying 'yes', even though we're not quite sure what things will look like."

"Love you, Dad," Audi smiled as she positioned a pillow against the car door and closed her eyes.

For most of my four years in San Diego, I honestly thought we would never leave the self-titled "America's Finest City." What had started in early 1995 as a true pioneering adventure to move out west had ended in humiliation, discouragement, and a sense of resignation. Unfortunately, Toni and I didn't really have a real clear sense that moving back was the "right thing to do." That was in strong contrast to the crisp sense of clarity, energy, and momentum we felt when we moved to San Diego. What we did know was that things weren't working well in San Diego for LifeVision, Inc. Alyssa (our oldest daughter) would be entering high school in the fall. Most of our family members lived in Illinois and Indiana. So, it was a decision based largely on practical factors, accompanied by a sense of frustration and defeat.

Leaving San Diego was one of the most difficult things we have ever done. My family and I said goodbye to great neighbors and coworkers, amazing friends, a lovely geographic area blessed with an abundance of the good stuff, and also to the sense of adventure that I felt for the entire time we had lived there. Heavy sigh. In many ways, I lived those years in San Diego with a sense of awe and wonderment, with the feeling that I was on vacation nearly every day. I was grateful to God for the opportunity to live in a beautiful place, with the ocean on one side and mountains on the other—and 70-degree year-round temps to boot!

Interestingly, I had a strange dream during the decision-making process to move back to Illinois. In the dream, I was taking furniture, appliances, and the like out of my house and putting them on the driveway. A neighbor stopped by to ask me what I was doing, and I replied, "That's the policy of the town, Mark—the stuff we got when we moved here has to be given back at some point. When the town council asks for it back, you have to put it on the driveway in preparation for the pickup crew to come by." And with that, I continued moving a variety of items out onto the driveway.

It was a very strange dream, indeed. Quite memorable for its weirdness—and yet upon waking the following morning, I was convinced I'd received a God-message. As I had wrestled to understand my failures and make sense of our decision to return to Illinois, perhaps God knew I needed some perspective, some reassurance that this decision was in a subtle way facilitated by him—or at least he was observing it carefully from the sidelines, like a coach, supporting and quietly rooting for me. Though the process was difficult, the dream gave me comfort that God shows up and is there in the middle of our most low moments—and that we have to trust him as we give back that which we thought was ours. Our time in San Diego had indeed been a gift, and now it was time to give the gift back, to put it out on the driveway.

I think that's the attitude with which we need to approach life and work—no matter how hard it is, as it was for us back then—to see each day and opportunity as a gift. To have the attitude of a steward, one caring for the assets of another, and to do our best with cultivating and developing the opportunities we are given. We don't know how long we'll have to develop and nurture each opportunity. We don't know when we'll be asked to give something away or release our grip and step back. But if we've honored the opportunity and done our best to offer it up to God along the way, we can have confidence that we've allowed our individual story to be integrated with God's story. And that is a holy, powerful thing.

In the 15 plus years since we left San Diego, many wonderful things have happened. Through the power of relationships that originated there, God has given us new perspective to and healing from our acute sense of loss in 1999. One of Toni's best friends, Shelley, moved from San Diego to Fort Worth a few years after we moved back to Illinois. Fort Worth happens to be 90 miles from where Audra and Kaley attended college (Baylor in Waco, Texas). So, the girls routinely drove up to Fort Worth to visit Shelley, Mark and their daughters, Marilyn and Jacilyn, their cul-de-sac playmates from San Diego. Alyssa, my oldest daughter, has maintained a lifelong friendship with Bethanny, whom she met in fifth grade in San Diego. Bethanny was one of Alyssa's bridesmaids in her wedding on August 6, 2011. I've been able to stay connected to our former pastor, Bill Jackson, and former accounting firm colleagues Ken Ritzman and Steve Austin. Toni has enjoyed her ongoing friendship with Angie Ritzman, Ken's wife. It really is encouraging that four short years could birth what have become lifelong relationships.

As painful and confusing as it was to leave San Diego (in fact, you'll see in the next chapter that we gave strong consideration to the idea of moving back to San Diego within the first year of being back in Illinois—oy vey!), I can now look back and believe that it was the right thing at the right time. The activating events and specific elements for making the decision to move back to Illinois in 1999 weren't nearly the same as those prompting the move to California in 1995. In fact, the two sets of circumstances were quite opposite, when you think about it. Yet there was a shared, fundamental principle of yielding ourselves to a higher purpose that we believed was at work in both circumstances. And the shared element of taking a risk through intentional acts of saying "yes" to God, to become part of the bigger story that I believe is unfolding for each of us.

Now, many years later, I can see that we've benefitted tremendously from our time there as well as our time back in Illinois. The passage of time and events has brought perspective and joy and a deep satisfaction that we've done our best to align our lives with God's bigger plan.

19. Just Do It

Chicago, Illinois
April 2005
vis a vis Champaign, Illinois
December, 1999

THERE WERE ABOUT FIVE MINUTES LEFT IN THE GAME. Illinois trailed Arizona by 14 points in the 2005 NCAA elite eight matchup at the Allstate Arena in Rosemont, Illinois. I turned to Steve and David on my right with a wistful look.

"I cannot believe this incredible season is ending like this," I said. "It's been a great run."

"Ranked number one since December 1," David said. "Expected to win it all in the NCAA tourney. And here we are on the brink of defeat." He looked as glum as I felt.

Steve shrugged. "What a season. I'm thrilled we got this far. Just couldn't quite get to the final destination." That destination, we all knew, was the Final Four—or perhaps even a national championship.

What unfolded over the next half hour was one of the most thrilling come-from-behind stories in the modern basketball era as Illinois somehow, someway tied the score in regulation. With utter disbelief on the faces of the Arizona Wildcat fans across from us in the arena, the overtime period belonged to Illinois with Dee Brown, Deron Williams, Luther Head, Roger Powell, James Augustine and their supporting cast propelling the University of Illinois Fighting Illini into the Final Four. The scene that followed the final buzzer can only be described as sports bedlam, with Illinois fans hugging complete strangers, arms oscillating wildly, and a decibel level that rivaled any sports setting I've ever encountered. The screams and whoops were deafening and exhilarating, creating a remarkable and unforgettable moment.

Within minutes of the team cutting down the nets and celebrating its unbelievable accomplishment, I was in the car with Steve and David, racing down I-57 toward Champaign. The cell phones were buzzing. Text messages were flying. The staff of our company in Champaign, Gameday Spirit, was screenprinting Final Four tee shirts as we drove, with mobs of fans lined up outside our Campustown store at Sixth and Green. With our store manager, Cory Shumard, and former owner/partner John Chisholm (who couldn't resist the opportunity to get in on the fun, though he no longer owned part of the company) seemingly in control of an uncontrollable situation at the Campustown store, Steve, David, and I decided to drive directly to the Illinois Athletics facilities where the basketball team was expected to arrive by 1 a.m. on Easter Sunday morning. Thousands of fans were already gathered there. When we popped open the hinged window to our Gameday merchandise trailer, we were overwhelmed with fans standing 10 deep and 10 wide, waiting to buy their souvenir Final Four shirt. The scene was unreal and forever etched in my memory as one of the wildest and most precious moments of my life.

So, how did we get there? How did a former accounting firm partner and failed LifeVision CEO become an owner of a "spirit store" for the University of Illinois? Well, I'd love to say that this particular opportunity and that the path to personal success in general have something to do with deft ability to foresee the future. Likewise, popular culture fancies the notion of the self-made person who achieves success through his or her own heroic, solo efforts, against spectacular odds. But my personal experience with the Gameday story bears testimony to something quite different. This is a story about a serendipitous opportunity that presented itself amidst a pretty difficult personal circumstance and one that pretty much defied conventional investment wisdom. This is a story about an opportunity, accompanied by a thoughtful decision process, the counsel of others, and ultimately about stepping out in faith to take a risk.

After moving back to Champaign, Illinois in June 1999, my good friend Steve Vogelsang asked me to assist him in selling his business. Gameday Spirit (then Gameday Sports), a merchandiser of Illini gear located on the University of Illinois campus, had been started by Steve in early 1998 when he purchased the assets of a failed retailer of sporting goods. Steve and his wife Stacie emptied out their savings account to make the initial purchase and then worked diligently to build their small business (talk about risk!). To say it was a tough slog is an understatement. Steve has related numerous stories of living on the edge that first year, getting as creative as possible to build a customer base and seeing only modest results. One of the key elements of his strategy was to win a merchandise concessions contract with the University of Illinois' Department of Intercollegiate Athletics. When that deal fell through, Steve sensed that it was time to pursue a full-time job elsewhere. That became the catalyst for selling Gameday.

While we explored several options for the potential sale of Gameday, nothing of substance was materializing. We contacted a variety of industry insiders—primarily folks running similar "spirit stores" at Big Ten universities. But the response was pretty lukewarm and nothing seemed to gel. In fact, the best alternative for liquidating the company was interest expressed by a national sandwich shop chain that wanted the lease rights to the store location, based in the heart of Campustown of the University of Illinois. We decided that if we could sell the lease rights for a decent price, we could then run a going-out-of-business sale to liquidate inventory. When it was all said and done, Steve might walk away with a couple hundred thousand in his pocket.

Basically, hardball tactics by the lawyer representing the sandwich shop chain made the process frustrating. So much so, that in the parking lot of the lawyer's office, Steve and I began throwing out the idea of him selling one-third of the business to me and one-third to John Chisholm, while he retained a one-third share. Each of us would keep our "day jobs," yet own Gameday on the side. Perfect solution, right? The only catch for me was coming up with $40,000 for my one-third share! My bank account had been depleted over the previous months from starting LifeVision, and as a result my family and I were experiencing a fair amount of financial difficulty. In fact, I had seen almost $100,000 of my personal savings evaporate over that time and had only $45,000 left in the bank!

I was very conflicted (obviously) about taking almost all of what I had left in savings to invest in a business where the founder was leaving to take another job! The scheme seemed rather harebrained, yet I couldn't put it aside. I gave the transaction a good deal of thought and prayer, and talked at length with my wife, Toni.

"So Steve and I went to talk to the lawyer for the sandwich chain today," I told her as we sat in our living room that evening. "Short story is, the deal fell through for selling them the lease rights."

"Oh, that's disappointing," she said. She was reading a magazine. "I know you thought that was the best option."

"Well, it was, until Steve and I got to thinking in the parking lot." I paused, not sure how she was going to take the next part.

"Yes, and…." Toni said, while she flipped the pages of her magazine.

"What do you think of the idea of us buying one-third of Gameday, the Chisholms buying one-third, and Steve keeping one-third? And we'd each keep our day jobs—running Gameday on the side."

It sounded crazy coming out of my mouth. I watched Toni carefully to see how she would react. She immediately stopped reading and raised an eyebrow.

"Buy one-third of Gameday. How much would that cost?"

"Forty grand." I hoped that somehow that would make it sound less serious than forty thousand.

"Forty thousand dollars?" Toni looked stunned. My ploy didn't work; she looked quite serious.

"Yes, forty grand," I replied, calmly. As if we were talking about buying a new grill I'd seen for about fifty bucks.

"And how much have we lost in the last two years with LifeVision?"

Ouch. Point-blank questions like that can hurt.

"Uh, well, I haven't added it up recently... maybe a hundred grand."

"You're the business guy here. How does this make sense? We've lost one hundred thousand in LifeVision, you've come close to quitting the business world altogether, and now you want to invest forty thousand in a tee shirt shop?"

Putting it like that made it sound pretty silly.

"Yes," I said quietly. If I couldn't win her over by slurring over money amounts, maybe meekness would work. I waited for her response.

"Well, let's see what God says in the next few days," she finally said. "I can't imagine that this deal make sense. But maybe he'll surprise us."

So, she wasn't totally ruling it out, then. The idea did seem like lunacy, although in the midst of it all, something about it seemed right, too. Perhaps Toni was signaling to me she had some small inkling that this deal could work.

What happened that following weekend was really quite strange. The only way I can characterize it is this: God showed up and spoke. Not directly, but through a trusted friend. Pam Larson, one of the pastors at the Vineyard Church in Urbana, approached me that Sunday after the service. She had no idea about the pending transaction or discussions that had been taking place between Steve and me, or the conversation that Toni and I had had just a few days prior.

"Tim, do you have a second to talk?" Pam asked.

"Sure. What's up?"

"Well, I've been thinking about you and Toni this week for some reason. As I prayed about you two, I sensed God giving me a specific word of direction for you. Are you facing a big decision of some kind?"

"Yes, as a matter of fact, we are." I left it at that, not wanting to divulge any of the specifics.

"Just do it."

"Excuse me—'just do it'—as in, we should say 'yes'?"

"Just do it. That's the message. I'll leave it up to you to decide what that means." She smiled, and as she walked away, a smile crept across my face.

Just do it.

It didn't take a detective to decipher the code. This phrase had a double meaning for me. It was an obvious nudge to do the deal, but nearly as importantly, this was Nike's main marketing slogan at the time—and Nike was the most prominent line of sportswear offered by Gameday. The message seemed undeniably clear to me.

So that following week, Toni and I decided to just do it, and bought a one-third interest in Gameday on December 1, 1999. With $45,000 in our savings account, we transferred $40,000 of it to Steve to finalize the deal. Let's just say it was no small risk to drain the bank account, yet as we signed the papers I felt a surge of faith that it would not just work out, but that we would receive an incredible return on our investment far beyond just a simple monetary return.

All these years later, Toni and I can indeed look back on what has been one of the most rewarding investments we have ever made. The business has returned many multiples our original investment amount. But perhaps more importantly, it has been one of the richest relational investments we have ever made. The Gameday business has provided us a great platform for interacting with topnotch college students, for making an impact in our local community by creating jobs and giving to causes like Coaches vs. Cancer, and for enjoying countless experiences with our fellow owners' families in the last decade plus. We've traveled together to out-of-state games, we've hosted employee Christmas parties in a family setting, and we enjoyed many unique experiences like the 2008 Rose Bowl with our nephew J Leman leading the Illinois defense. And, the thrill of experiencing the 2005 Final Four just may have been the "business highlight" of the decade for me!

In moments of quiet reflection, I sometimes think to myself, what would have happened if I hadn't stepped out and taken the risk to buy Gameday? What would be missing from life today, without the countless special moments Toni and I got to share with our co-owners and friends? Who would we have missed the opportunity to impact? How would our family have been different? It doesn't take me long to offer a prayer of gratitude to God for nudging me over the edge to "just do it" all those years ago.

20. All that Glitters?

La Jolla, California
May 2000

I REMEMBER FRED STANDING AWKWARDLY IN THE DOORWAY TO MY OFFICE with his right hand seeming to hold the doorframe from caving in. His angled body language told me he was an unhappy camper. I'd just told him that as much as I wanted to work things out, and as diligently as we had all tried over the previous five months, I had decided that our business deal was off. I wouldn't be moving back to San Diego to spearhead the new division of Fred's company.

"So, we've all invested a lot of hours and a ton of effort in working on this, but you're throwing in the towel?" Fred said.

"I know it's a big disappointment for you and Bill, and it is for me too," I replied.

"Well, I just don't understand."

"I don't expect you to fully understand. It's not been an easy decision by any stretch—but I'm convinced that breaking up our business 'engagement' will be far better and less costly than getting a divorce down the road."

Fred sighed. Frustration seemed to ooze from his pores. "So, what's the bottom line?" he asked coldly. "How did you decide that this wasn't going to work?"

"Well, although I'm excited about the vision that you and Bill have for this new division, and as much as I believe I have the skills and experience needed to do this job, I've sensed in the last month that the three of us just aren't in alignment with each other."

Fred's cheeks colored. He stopped leaning against the doorframe and stood up straight, glaring at me. "Not in alignment?! That sounds like some pretty interesting consulting-speak. Just what does that mean?"

"What I mean is, at the most fundamental level, we don't agree on the vision for this potential new enterprise," I said. "And our values—the things most important as we build it—are not in synch with each other."

So started a difficult and lengthy conversation between Fred and me—one that was as uncomfortable as any I can remember. I'm not sure I communicated clearly on this difficult topic, one wrapped in plenty of emotion for both of us. I had really wanted to make this work, but I knew deep down that I would be making a big mistake. Just five months before, in January of 2000, this opportunity seemed to have the hallmarks of a great fit. Indeed, it offered a welcome drink of water in what had been a year and a half drought in my business career.

I had spent the previous 18 months trying to make a go of it in LifeVision, Inc. I had begun the company in San Diego, and with multiple failures compounding one another, we had moved back to Champaign, Illinois, in June of 1999. What I had hoped would be a fresh start in Illinois turned out to be more of the same—challenge, failure, disappointment. As the year wound down, I reached my lowest point—and as I shared earlier, almost opted out of the professional business world altogether. But my brother Ben had given me enough encouragement to hang in there just a bit longer. He was convinced that the tide would turn.

And sure enough, during the first week of January, I received what appeared to be a very attractive offer that came from two businessmen in San Diego. Fred and Bill (not their real names) were operating a franchise organization that worked with executives across the country. Their business model was pretty successful, but they were interested in delivering more value to their franchisees, and that's where I came in.

With my consulting background in an international accounting firm, Fred and Bill were interested in my help to develop and deliver consulting and training tools to their franchisees. So when I got the call to consider flying out to San Diego that January, I was intrigued and excited. The potential seemed promising, particularly considering everything that had gone down in the previous year and a half. (In retrospect, perhaps my sense of discernment wasn't functioning too well!)

From January through May, I made a number of trips to California. Fred, Bill, and I worked diligently on putting together a strategic plan to create a Consulting Services Division of their business. As the process unfolded, Fred and Bill consistently affirmed that my background and experience were a good fit for the new business segment of their core franchisee offering. Having lived in the San Diego area from 1995 to 1999, there was a strong pull to go back to a place that I dearly loved. Perhaps that factor, more than anything else, kept me driving forward. I wasn't paying much attention to the small red flags along the way. Overall, the pieces of the puzzle—the business model, the strategy, the product offerings and such—were falling into place quite nicely.

Throughout the five months of working together, however, I did begin to have some doubts. Amidst all of the trees of strategic plans, budgets, and day-to-day work, I felt a nagging sense that the forest had some fundamental problems. One of the seminal moments in this process was a focus group session we conducted in April, 2000, to present the business model and some of the specific tools we'd been putting together to a group of potential customers, advisors, and friends. During this experience, I began to understand why I'd been so uneasy in the previous few weeks. A lunchtime conversation with my good friend Kevin Peterson helped to further clarify things. Kevin had a deep background in organization development and leadership training, and was presently operating as an independent contractor offering his services to large organizations. I was excited that he'd agreed to fly into San Diego to participate in the session.

"Great morning session, Tim," Kevin said as he reached for his tuna sandwich. "I especially liked the part about strategic planning tools. I could use some of those tools myself."

"Thanks, Kevin. I really appreciate you taking the time to attend the focus group." I took a sip of my iced tea and looked over Kevin's shoulder for a moment. I must have had a glazed look in my eye.

"You okay?" Kevin asked.

"Yeah, I'm fine," I said. "It's just that something's been rumbling around inside of me this morning. Something I hadn't seen before, not this clearly." The intuition that was growing in me came with a vague sense of dread. I wasn't sure how to frame it, but Kevin prodded me to try.

"Such as?"

"Well, to be blunt, I think I'm not in alignment with Bill, Fred, and their company. Sounds a little crazy, I know, since we've been working so hard on getting it going. But there it is."

Kevin shrugged. "It's not crazy if it's real. Why do you think you're not aligned with them?"

I thought about this for a moment. "I think, to be honest, some of the most basic parts of the foundation are seriously out of whack. This is all sort of crystalizing for me in real time. I think the execution path they envision is fundamentally different from the one I envision."

"Sounds pretty serious to me."

I nodded and then shook my head. "I'd say it's really serious. What's becoming clear to me is this: I would only be the one in charge of this new division on paper. In reality, Fred and Bill would micromanage me. Bill's talk on strategic vision this morning confirmed that."

We ate in silence for a few moments with that heavy statement hanging in the air between us. The mood had become quite somber. I could tell Kevin was concerned for me.

"So," Kevin finally said, "what are you going to do?"

I raised an eyebrow and gave him a tight smile. "Good question," I said. "Either I take the plunge and work with these guys—or I pull the plug."

I discovered later that a common theme in organizational behavior and culture is a mismatch between personal values and goals (mine in this case) and those of a company (Fred and Bill's, as the managing partners) often leads to disaster. Bret Simmons, PhD, an experienced researcher of positive organizational behavior and leadership, says this about alignment of personal and company values: "One of the things new research suggests that enhance engagement is value congruence. Value congruence is the extent to which the individual can behave at work consistent with their own self-image. It's very difficult to experience meaningfulness in our work if we are expected to behave in ways that are inconsistent with the highest values we espouse to ourselves and others." This is a fairly accurate description of the reasoning why I felt I couldn't continue on with Bill and Fred.

Although I had pinpointed why I couldn't continue forward with this company, it was extremely disappointing to realize that months of effort and expense were coming to naught. Even more upsetting, I had set my heart on the idea of moving back to the San Diego area (as had my family!). I was so sure that this was going to work, that we had even gone to the lengths of listing our home for sale and hiring a realtor in San Diego to help us find a home there. And we'd spread the news to family and friends in the Champaign area that we were once again moving to California. In the end, we decided to put the kibosh on the whole deal. Fred, Bill, and I agreed to go our separate ways, we pulled our house off the market in Champaign, and I tucked my tail back between my legs.

Many years later, I'm still not entirely sure why those five months in early 2000 happened the way they did. I guess one of the simple lessons from this experience is to date before you marry. Metaphorically speaking, I am grateful that we had a few months of courting before deciding to move forward with a business marriage that likely would have ended up in divorce. In reflecting on this experience, I'm convinced that it is critical for business partners to be on the same page from a mission, vision, and values perspective, right from the start. Too many great ideas go up in flames because the fundamental relationships just aren't in good alignment with one another.

When I work with entrepreneurs or teams of people who are contemplating the launch of a business venture, I encourage them to think carefully through these foundational matters of core values, mission, and vision before entering a business relationship with other parties—be they partners, vendors, or investors. This is particularly true in any new entrepreneurial endeavor. Sometimes the excitement of forming a new company with cool technology and great market opportunity can obscure a faulty foundation of misalignment of the team. It is worth the effort to probe beneath the surface of a potential business deal or project, asking the key questions that address core values, mission and vision. Questions such as:

- Mission: Does the business or project have a clearly defined "reason for being"? Has the business identified need in the marketplace, currently unmet, that can be satisfied by the offering of the new business? If so, what is it?
- Vision: Does the business or project have a specific picture of a where it wants to be in three to five years? If so, what is it and, generally speaking, how will it get there? Is there agreement among the team of what the vision looks like?
- Values: How will the new business "do business"? Or, what are the basic guidelines for how business will be conducted by the new enterprise? Have those values been articulated and if so, what are they? If not, why not?
- How do the personal mission, vision, and values of each of the people involved with the project or business align with the above three questions? Is there harmony, or are there gaps?
- How do the personal mission, vision, and values of each team member align with each other? Where are the potential problem spots?

At the end of the day, taking time to explore alignment is well worth the investment and effort—and it may well save you from heartache and disappointment in the end.

21. A Temporary Stopover

San Diego, California
September 2001
vis a vis Champaign, Illinois
May, 2000

THE EVENING AIR WAS PLEASANTLY COOL. As I sat on a bench along the boardwalk, watching the moonlight bounce off the small ripples in San Diego Bay, I lit a cigar and turned my thoughts heavenward. It's one of my favorite ways to pray, actually—with a cigar on the back deck of my home, or in this particular case, watching the harbor ferries pass by. So for the next hour of that evening, I had a conversation with God about the future, about doubts and hopes, about my desire for meaningful relationships and work. It was a peaceful and cathartic process.

Having flown in earlier that morning, I was a day ahead of the rest of the SourceGear Corporation team, who were scheduled to arrive early the next day. We were preparing to exhibit at the CTIA Wireless Show (originally, CTIA stood for Cellular Telephone Industry Association, but it now represents a broader range of wireless companies and technologies). SourceGear would be unveiling a new wireless application we had created called Baby Air Link—a piece of software that would enable parents with sick children to communicate directly with their healthcare providers and receive real-time updates. Sound like 2014? Actually, the date was September 10, 2001.

I was awakened the next morning by Toni calling my cell phone.

"Are you up yet, honey? You've got to turn on the TV, now!"

Glancing at the alarm clock, I saw that it was about 6:30 am. "What can be so important on TV at this hour? And, what channel?"

"Any channel. Turn it on, now."

I could immediately sense from the raw emotion in her voice that something very serious was going down. Still a bit groggy, I found the remote on the nightstand and flipped it on. There I was confronted with startling images of the Twin Towers, both on fire with massive amounts of billowing smoke pouring from them. And although most of us did not fully understand it that morning, for the next few hours we were participants in the most profound moment of the young 21st century. The World Trade Center was burning and ultimately collapsed; the Pentagon had been attacked; another airliner was reported down in Pennsylvania. The depth and breadth of these events would utterly change life as we knew it.

The SourceGear team that planned to join me had been on a TWA flight departing St. Louis, taxiing for takeoff. They were called back to the terminal, just as the no-fly order was issued by the FAA. The CTIA Wireless Show attempted to go on, but better than half of the exhibitors had not set up their displays. A gala event, scheduled for opening night on the 11th, became a communal grieving, coping, questioning, television-watching exercise with the big screen set up in the auditorium. We grappled with the unbelievable. We were saddened and shocked beyond words. For years to come, the reverberations of the horrible events from that morning would be felt in nearly every arena of human experience.

From a business perspective, I did not anticipate much impact—but I was in fact, quite wrong. Over the next several weeks, SourceGear's business began to dramatically slow. What had already been a challenging year (think Internet bubble, wireless, and telecom industry shake-ups in 2001) became almost the complete undoing of a successful company. Because most of SourceGear's business had something to do with these industries, we experienced a significant downturn in our business. So, during the waning weeks of 2001, the company's founder and I decided I would step down from the SourceGear presidency, we would lay off a wave of folks from all levels of the company, and we would put a survival plan in place.

I hated to see these things happen to SourceGear and its people. And I hated to leave. But there really was no choice. World events had combined with very practical everyday stuff to force our hand. I had learned so much in the previous 20 months of my tenure there—and most importantly, I had regained my footing after the very difficult years preceding it. As I prepared to depart the company, I reflected back with some fondness on what God had taught me in my brief time there. I had expected to stay for while, but as it turned out, SourceGear ended up being only a brief stop-over on my entrepreneurial journey. In that short time, he had perfectly prepared me for my next adventure.

My stint with SourceGear started off with an unexpected job offer from my good friend Eric Sink, the company founder and CEO, in May, 2000. The offer came on the heels of the five-month experiment with Fred and Bill (Chapter 20) that had left me frustrated, to say the least. After nearly two years of failure and uncertainty about what the future for me and my family held, the possibility of taking a stable position with a growing company was a godsend indeed. I recall the conversation very well.

"Tim, do you have a minute?" Eric asked. He had wandered into my office, one of three nondescript 10-by-12 spaces our consulting firm was subletting from SourceGear. Eric had graciously allowed us to lease the space for pretty much next to nothing. He knew our fledgling consulting firm, LifeVision, was struggling.

"Sure. What's on your mind?"

"SourceGear has grown pretty rapidly in the last couple of years, and I think we're at the point of needing someone to help us with strategy and finances. I see sunny days ahead, but only if someone is helping us put in some structure and discipline beforehand."

"Well, I know some folks that could fill the bill. Would you like their names?" I asked.

"To be honest, Tim, I was thinking of you. Are you in the market for something like this?"

I felt a cold shudder on the nape of my neck. Was I being offered a job? After a couple years of futility and a recently failed effort to return to San Diego?

"I'm listening," I responded.

He went on to tell me more about the company and his needs, and how he envisioned me fitting in, and ended by saying, "I think you're the perfect person for the job. How does a position as controller or CFO of SourceGear grab you?"

I took a deep breath and plunged in. "Controller, CFO, not so much—because I think your needs are bigger than that, from what I can see," I replied.

I knew I was taking a risk. Here I was being offered a job, an opportunity to find some stability and to have my sense of self-worth restored. And yet I was telling him "No, but…." What was I thinking?

"So what do you think my needs are, then?" Eric looked rather puzzled.

"I'm thinking you need a president to come along side you as CEO and really make this thing hum. And for good measure, I'll do the CFO job too, because I think I can do them both well."

There was a pause, during which I held my breath. Maybe I'd pushed too far.

"I think you're right, Tim. So, how about the position of president and CFO, then?"

I grinned, exhaled, and told him that sounded great. Within a few days, we had worked out an agreement for me to join SourceGear as its president and CFO.

Eric had founded SourceGear a few years earlier, and the company had experienced excellent growth by early 2000. SourceGear offered tools for software developers, and it also had a custom contracting division doing internet browser work for cell phones and personal digital assistants (the precursors of today's smart phones). While wireless apps number in the tens of thousands today, there were almost none just a decade ago. A true Internet and wireless pioneer, Eric and his team at Spyglass (his predecessor company) had written the first versions of what became Microsoft Internet Explorer, based on the University of Illinois' Mosaic browser technology. Nearly all of the SourceGear employees were technical in nature, with a couple of "non-techies" doing some accounting and administrative work.

My consulting firm, LifeVision, had done some work for Eric, and we'd known each other personally since the mid 1980s. And over the course of several months in 1999 and 2000, as a tenant in Eric's building, we'd become pretty well acquainted with each others' goings-on. So in terms of the proposed idea of working together as an executive team, there seemed to be very good alignment on several fronts. As we worked through the terms of our deal, I was very encouraged. And we wasted no time in getting after it. Together, we immediately began to implement a strategy to support and nurture the growth that was occurring. Eventually, the staff of about 22 would grow to just shy of 40. We began implementing the systems and procedures of a "grown-up company."

While there were many exciting days at SourceGear, and the company seemed poised for significant growth and a bright future, there were two challenges that confronted me on an almost-daily basis. The first is what I now call "the power of a technology-centric culture." In short, from the time I came into the company, there was an undercurrent of resistance to "business management" from some of the charter members of the technology team. On one of my management-by-walking-around visits, I had the following conversation with Roger (not his real name):

"Tim, you seem like a good guy and all, and I appreciate Eric's desire to upgrade our professionalism around here," Roger started out—a great backhanded compliment if ever there was one.

"I sense there is a 'but' in there, Roger. Go on."

"Well, SourceGear is a successful company because of its technology, right? Adding 'management' to it may help a bit, but, to be honest, I personally think it matters very little what management does or doesn't do."

Okay then. Don't hold back, Roger. Let your true feelings out.

"So, you think business management is essentially window dressing, then?"

Roger shrugged, but he didn't look a bit apologetic. "I know it hurts to hear that, Tim—but that's a fair assessment. Whether a software company ultimately performs has everything to do with its technology and almost nothing to do with management."

I waited to see if he had any more shots to fire, but he just looked at me. I gave him a slight smile and a nod. "Okay. Thanks for the insight, Roger. I appreciate your time."

He shrugged again and turned back to his computer. He looked a bit disappointed, as if he had hoped I would apologize for sucking money from the company and resign on the spot.

Now, it would be one thing if this was the perspective of a single employee. But I soon discovered that Roger was just the most vocal with his sentiments. In fact, the thoughts he shared with me (perhaps he was their designated spokesperson?) were representative of most of the software engineering team. And in the fourteen years since this conversation with Roger, I've encountered dozens of scientists and technologists with pretty much this same mindset. It varies a bit from person to person—but at the core, it translates to "that which is empirical, technical, scientific, and tangible has value; that which is interpersonal, nontechnical, business-oriented and intangible is, relatively speaking, worth much less." Of course, not every scientist and engineer subscribes to this philosophy. But when a businessperson is blessed with one or more members of her team who think this way, the task of leadership can be particularly difficult.

The other element of SourceGear that I found quite challenging was the "power of a founder-centric culture." Eric was and is one of the most brilliant professionals I've ever had the pleasure to work with. His technical team loved and respected him. Because so much of the workforce was technical, the prevailing sentiment in the company was "Eric is the boss." That's great on one hand—employee loyalty and commitment can lead to a very successful future for a company. However, this made it pretty tough for the new president on the block to effectively execute his job.

Not surprisingly, this type of situation happens quite frequently in the business world. A business professional who enters a company as a key figure after a culture has been established is often met with hostility and an opposition to change, and experiences trouble earning the respect and trust of her new subordinates. The new leader must make a concerted effort to resolve this dilemma by making immediately valuable contributions, demonstrating visible successes, working hard at building relationships with key people, and earning the respect and trust of the team.

These two lessons—the power of a technology-centric culture and the power of a founder-centric culture—proved to be invaluable in the next leg of my business journey. Though my stop-over at SourceGear was short in the big scheme of things, it was the ideal preparation for launching into the next venture—iCyt Mission Technology, a technology company building cell measurement instruments for disease researchers.

With the iCyt opportunity, our founding team had a blank canvas from which to create a new way of doing business. If we were able to do it well, we could create a culture that would honor the contributions of technologists and businesspeople from the very beginning. And, we could create a company that was not founder-centric—indeed, our heart was to make it employee- and customer-centric. As we began in late 2001 to map out the vision for what would become iCyt, it was encouraging that our core team was on the same page regarding the kind of company we wanted to create. iCyt would be a company that would honor God. It would solve big problems in disease research. And, importantly, iCyt would be a place where we as leaders honored all of our employees and their respective contributions.

22. 20/20 Vision

Anaheim, California
December 2009
Vis a vis Champaign, Illinois
February, 2001

I WAS STANDING IN LINE AT THE FINDING NEMO SUBMA-RINE VOYAGE RIDE at Disneyland with about 618 of my closest friends, snaking along very, very slowly. My cell phone rang. It was John Banta, the executive director of Illinois Ventures and a fellow board member of iCyt Mission Technology. John calmly explained that there were some last-minute things going down that required us to make quick decisions or the transaction to sell the company to Sony Corporation would not happen as scheduled tomorrow.

Of course. Did I expect anything different at that stage of the game? Always expect the unexpected, they say, but this one caused me a bit more anxiety than most "unexpecteds." I appreciated John's serene demeanor as he talked me through last-minute details that were impacting the transaction to the tune of several hundred thousand dollars. After all, it's only money, right? His composure helped me to refrain from grabbing the light sabre from the little kid in front of me and start swinging.

Forty-five minutes later the issues were settled with an ad-hoc board meeting. Eighteen hours later the deal was done. iCyt had become a Sony Corporation company, and our little bio-instrument start-up had experienced (in venture capital lingo) a successful exit. So closed a chapter in my entrepreneurial trek that had begun nearly nine years before.

In February of 2001, at the urging of my brother-in-law and pastor, Happy Leman, I scheduled lunch with a fellow Vineyard Church member whom I knew only in passing. Hap explained to me that this fellow churchgoer, who was a scientist at the University of Illinois (he prefers not to be identified in this book), had "a potential business opportunity" he wanted to discuss. Of course I said yes, disregarding the fact that most of the folks Hap had sent my way over the years turned into free advice sessions that didn't amount to much in the end. One can only endure so many free lunches.

But over salads at Chili's on North Prospect in Champaign, I learned that this was indeed a legitimate, and fascinating, business opportunity. Monsanto (the Fortune 50 agricultural conglomerate known by most as the maker of Roundup herbicide) was interested in developing "gender-enriched semen" as a product to be sold in the dairy industry. The basic idea was to offer dairy farmers, at a premium price, straws of bull semen that had been processed to sort out the Y's and keep the X's, hence increasing the odds of birthing a cow instead of a bull. They'd been working on the idea for a couple of years without much success and had concluded that perhaps they needed some outside expertise to assist in developing this new product idea.

I shared my perspective with my lunch companion regarding the necessary elements to building a successful business partnership with a company like Monsanto—with a fair amount of warning that starting something from scratch was not for the faint of heart. Based on the challenges I was experiencing in my day job at SourceGear, it wasn't a stretch to say that cutting-edge technology alone would not "cut it." There would be several other key ingredients required for sustained success. And anything truly worth doing should be carefully planned to include these other ingredients from the beginning, all while building toward long-term success.

Alone with my thoughts that afternoon, I wondered if I'd been exposed to "just another good idea" or whether this opportunity might actually go somewhere. If it did go somewhere, should I become involved? And if involved, how involved? After all, I had a day job and things seemed to be going reasonably well. I took out a blank sheet of paper, jotted down a few thoughts of how I would approach Monsanto's problem, and spent some time doodling (I'm still quite fond of that brainstorming technique today!). As late afternoon approached, I put the paper away and mused that this was something that could quite possibly come around down the road.

Several months later, in the fall of 2001, that "something" did indeed come around. I recall standing in the break room at SourceGear, the company that rented space to our part-time consulting business, LifeVision. I took a Diet Pepsi from the refrigerator and a bag of peanuts from the snack box, then turned around to find my LifeVision partner entering the room.

"Hey, John, do you have a few minutes?" I motioned to the chairs in front of us.

"Sure, Tim, what've you got?" John replied, as he grabbed a soda and sat down.

"This Monsanto project that you and I have been assisting on definitely has legs. The team has put together a strong proposal for Monsanto to consider, and I think there's a high likelihood that they'll buy it. If that happens, there will be a dozen engineers to hire, about 4,000 square feet of space to lease, supplies and equipment to be bought, accounting systems to put in place—basically this would be the birth of a new company."

"Sounds exciting!"

"Yes, it does—definitely. But now I'm personally at a real crossroads."

"Tell me about it," John said. It was times like this that I really appreciated John's genuine care and concern for me.

"So far, I've been contributing to this project as a consultant in my spare, non-SourceGear time. But with the odds seeming likely that Monsanto will want to move forward, I think the scope of my involvement could dramatically increase. Someone is going to have to tend to all of these business details, not to mention the more complicated aspects of developing a sound business strategy to tie the pieces together. I'm tempted to be that guy—my mind is already working on the specifics of how this could all come together. But before I get too far, I need to make a decision—take a leap of faith on this and be the business guy, or stand on the sidelines as a cheerleader."

"Both options sound ok to me," John said, a twinkle in his eye. "Which one do you think God is directing you to consider?"

"That's the $64,000 question. I just don't know. But I'm eager to find out."

We continued chatting for a while, laying out the pluses and minuses of moving forward. Ultimately, I had to answer some tough questions. Did this emerging opportunity really fit with my sense of personal purpose? Was it aligned with my core values? And, did it move me closer to achieving my vision of the future? These were the fundamental questions that begged answers before we moved on to the strategic, operational, and tactical questions behind the creation of a business. So often, entrepreneurs focus on the latter and forget the former. Bad idea.

So for the next couple of weeks, I asked myself different versions of these tough questions. Was this opportunity a distraction or something really congruent with my understanding of my purpose? Was I willing to invest considerable time and risk failure for the potential upside of this deal? Could I find the passion and determination to really go all in on this opportunity? Was the timing right, relative to the other things happening in my life? And, perhaps most importantly for me, did the iCyt opportunity resonate with what I sensed was God's call on my life?

With SourceGear struggling as 2001 was coming to a close, there was some interesting appeal to the iCyt opportunity. The fact that my tenure at SourceGear was winding down and iCyt was presenting itself was either highly coincidental, or it was God. The mental and emotional gymnastics were pretty intense. Only a few years prior, I'd left the big accounting firm and started LifeVision. Two years of failure, including a crazy five months of finagling a business deal to potentially move back to San Diego, had led me to SourceGear. While a nice landing spot, the SourceGear job was now on shaky ground. The events of 9/11 had put a major whammy on our business. So was this the right next thing for me? Did it fit with the calling on my life? Was it really time to make another risky move and join the team to launch iCyt?

The answers to these tough questions came up "yes" for me. Not a terribly clear yes, but a yes nonetheless. So with no small amount of fear and trepidation, it was time for me to take another risk-filled leap to assist in actualizing the vision of iCyt. It may have helped that my attitude was "I'll give this a solid two-year commitment, and then we'll see what happens. If nothing else, I'll learn a lot in the process." In fact, that mindset may have been the necessary factor in pushing me over the decision edge.

About the time I settled the issue in my heart, Monsanto came knocking—saying "yes" to the complete, turnkey solution to their problem that we had proposed. The proposal was bold and risky, some might say audacious—because we were offering to solve their problem with a team that didn't quite exist, that would work together in a facility that was yet to be leased, with systems that were yet to be established and equipment yet to be bought. In short, we were long on intangibles. But what we did have was the founding team's vision, passion, and commitment to make the company and Monsanto's project a success. And, most importantly, a solid sense of God's calling and favor on this particular moment in our personal stories and his blessing on the vision to create a company that would solve big problems in an employee-honoring, fun, and exciting way.

And in retrospect, it was crucial that these elements were in place in order for iCyt to succeed in the long run. Had the team not been committed—passionate, determined, aligned, and called—I'm not sure we would have successfully weathered the considerable challenges that would soon come our way.

23. Have You Seen the Lyt?

Del Mar, California
April 2003

I WAS SLOGGING THROUGH MY THIRD SALES TRIP OF THE MONTH, this one on the west coast. Each of my previous trips had started with great enthusiasm and amped anticipation of success—only to end in disappointment. Fly and then thud, as my wife Toni is fond of saying. I was peddling iCyt's new solid-state laser system, the Lyt Laser, to research hospitals, institutes, and universities. The Lyt was a state-of-the-art replacement for water-cooled, three-phase-power, argon-ion lasers—an integral component to biological cell sorting instruments. The Lyt offered exceptional performance, a footprint that was a small fraction that of argon-ion lasers, and it operated with wall-plug-in power with no need for expensive water-cooling apparatus. The offering was compelling, at least in my humble opinion! And certainly the technology should sell itself.

Reality check. iCyt was a new, unknown company, competing against the well-established titans of cytometry industry. Now, just who are you guys again? Headquartered in Champaign, Illinois? Where is that exactly? Well, thank you so much for the opportunity to review your cool technology. Don't let the door hit you in the backside as you exit.

I had just returned to the Stratford Inn, a one-star hotel/motel in Del Mar, California, with a partial view of the Pacific Ocean. It had been a long, exhausting, and disappointing day. The two meetings I had scheduled were a bust; one got cancelled and the other ended up being a tire-kicker. I was sitting on a bench underneath a pine tree, with scents of eucalyptus wafting through the ocean-breeze air.

But the lovely surroundings and rugged beauty in the coastal landscape were hard to appreciate. I found myself struggling, pondering what it would take to make my efforts a success. I thought we had a strategy that made sense: We were bringing powerful technology to the marketplace, pricing it just right, offering exceptional service, meanwhile gussying it up in a beautiful package and creating some well-done marketing fliers. We had figured, voila, the cytometry world will beat a path to our door! Success was easily within our reach.

Hmmm. Didn't happen that way. Note to budding technology entrepreneurs: Great technology, in itself, does not a commercial success make. Even surrounding technology with great sales and marketing, sharp people, business infrastructure, and a well conceived strategic plan does not guarantee success. While these things all increase the odds of success, an entrepreneurial endeavor is always confronting risk and dealing with ambiguity in some form or fashion. And when you're taking risks, there is always the chance of failure.

iCyt had launched in late 2001 in response to the unique opportunity to build a specialized cell-handling instrument for Monsanto Company. Monsanto's interest had to do with creating a special product by using the iCyt instrument that would be targeted for the dairy industry. As such, the contract with Monsanto permitted iCyt to develop a parallel technology for cell sorting and handling that could be offered to the disease research market, in which they had no interest.

The project to build these instruments would take several years and several million dollars. If everything went as planned (which it never does in business!), we would have commercial instruments available in

2006 or 2007, we estimated. Our hope was to become a significant force in the cytometry industry, which simply put, is the study and practice of cell analysis and manipulation for a variety of healthcare, agricultural, and other scientific purposes.

We knew that it would be important to create some market awareness, and hopefully some customer familiarity with iCyt, ahead of our introduction of this state-of-the-art cell sorting technology. Ideally, we would do this a couple of years in advance, so as to greatly enhance the introduction of our game-changing instrument when it was ready for the market.

We found just the way to do it, with the creation and roll-out of the Lyt laser system. The thinking at the time was, we will bring the Lyt to market, build a solid base of customers in the cytometry industry, and prove to the market that iCyt can produce and sell and service a quality instrument system. Then, when we were ready to bring our major instrument (later called the Reflection cell sorter) to the market, customers will know us, love us, and be ready to buy it!

The Lyt had been designed and engineered in cooperation with Coherent Laser, located in Santa Clara, California, and the engineering/development project had proven to be exciting. The performance of the technology was exceptional. The opportunity seemed ripe, and we felt ready to take on the world. The problem was, we had vastly underestimated the difficulty of bringing a new product to the market in a well-established industry with well-entrenched competitors. Customers were leery of this upstart company located in the middle of the corn and soybean fields of the Midwest. Would our company survive the odds that are stacked against start-ups and be there a year or two from now? Would we be able to provide the same or better level of service that our much larger competitors offered? Would the technology, cutting-edge as it was, work consistently and as well as the older, more established instruments?

We ran into roadblocks of every conceivable kind. One high-profile cancer center used our demonstrator system for two months, with the agreement to purchase it if the performance was solid. At the end of two months, they did agree to buy it, but for half price! That sale fell through. Another customer who used our demonstrator got the sale approved through several channels, only to have it fall apart at the last sign-off. Another potential customer agreed to put the demonstrator in, but when we ran into installation snafus with the demo, he backed out. Finally, a national lab agreed to purchase one, but only if we could work out a custom leasing arrangement with a series of one-year leases, which was very complicated and risky for us, but a deal we did end up doing, in fact.

Three months of crisscrossing the country in attempts to sell our Lyt laser had been fruitless. In that time, we had tallied one sale! This was frustrating on any number of levels, as I firmly believed we had "done things right" in building a great product that did indeed outperform existing competitive offerings. We had backed the system with a solid warranty. We had offered demonstrator units at no charge. Sometimes, you can do everything right, so to speak, but still end up with lackluster results.

In the middle of this less-than-spectacular product launch, a good friend, Dick Riffle, motioned me over from across the Vineyard Church lobby.

"So I hear you've hit some snags bringing your new product to market," Dick said.

I told him we indeed had, and we weren't sure why or which direction to go next.

"Sounds really frustrating," Dick said. "I don't know anything about lasers, so I won't offer you any business advice. But I would like to make you an offer."

"Sure, fire away."

"How about if we meet once a week to pray and ask for God's intervention and direction? Would that help?" Dick asked.

"We've tried everything else!" I smiled.

And so, we took Dick up on his offer, and for the next few months, met on Tuesday afternoons and "pounded on heaven," as we called it. There were no immediate results, but the process was cathartic and seemed to boost our flagging spirits. To know that a friend, with no direct connection to our business and with nothing financial to gain, would offer to join us in resolving our conundrum was encouraging, humbling, and energizing.

And, then the pattern of disappointment, roadblocks, and No's broke. Our months of prayer were answered toward the end of summer of 2003 as a trickle of sales emerged in August. More unit orders followed that fall, at an increasing pace. Then late that year, the biggest break of all came when a very large instrument company signed an OEM arrangement with us whereby the Lyt would be incorporated into their instrument system. Once that deal was inked, the floodgates swung open.

Eventually, we sold several hundred Lyt laser systems at an average unit price in the low $30 thousand range, and we did indeed accomplish what we had set out to do. The cytometry world became familiar with iCyt. They knew we were capable of producing a high-quality product. They knew we were there to service and stand behind our products. And when we did introduce the Reflection cell-sorting instrument in 2006, a large part of its success was due to the Lyt laser having paved the way. Ultimately, iCyt attracted the attention and interest of Sony Corporation, and we were sold to them in late 2009, due in no small part to the Lyt laser.

In retrospect, what had started out as an interesting idea to help us build some credibility in the marketplace turned out to be a critical success factor in the growth of iCyt. The cash generated from Lyt laser sales was a real boon to our young company, and helped us postpone venture capital funding for a number of years until our company valuation had grown substantially. Yet the market acceptance of our laser device was less than stellar—er, nonexistent—for nearly a half year. What would have happened if we'd given up? How would the story have unfolded if Dick hadn't encouraged us to seek God's direction and help?

Fortunately, we were able to push through a very difficult beginning to the Lyt product launch, make some customer-focused changes, and ultimately see success. Reflecting on that challenging period of multiple rejections in the first half of 2003, I learned several key business lessons:

- Various challenges you don't anticipate will occur (regardless of splendid plans and wonderful products),
- Resilience in the face of those challenge is absolutely necessary (if you don't get back up after getting knocked down, you're likely to get run over), and
- Good things can happen to those who believe in their business solutions and are passionate about bringing it to market.

Most importantly, though, I learned that pounding on heaven in concert with a good friend—even with no observable short-term results—can be the real difference maker. Thank you, Dick Riffle (and may you rest in peace)!

24. Rest

Champaign, Illinois
May 2008

From our seats in the open-air restaurant in Budapest, I could see the moonlight reflecting off the Danube River. With the light emanating from the buildings perched on the bluff across the river, it was a million-dollar view. Everything made the evening seem magical.

Well, nearly everything. The dinner conversation I was having with Fred Molnar, iCyt's vice president of sales, brought me back to earth.

Fred and I were in Budapest for the International Society of Analytical Cytology conference and trade show. It was "the" event in our industry, held every two years, alternating between the US and Europe. Our flagship product, the Reflection cell sorter, was being showcased on the international stage—and we were taking it by storm. The crowds had been lined deep in our spacious, well-appointed display area. There was an unmistakable energy that each of us experienced that week, with our US team joined by a dealer from Israel and a technical rep from the Czech Republic. It was a rewarding experience made even more memorable with its setting in Budapest, a city with hundreds of years of history oozing from its streets, buildings, and people.

Now, at dinner, I took a bite of my goulash and looked up to see a pained expression on Fred's face.

"Tim, I just don't get it. How could you be thinking about leaving iCyt? It doesn't make sense to me." Fred forcefully plunked his knife on the table as if to put an exclamation mark on his comments.

I took a deep breath and looked him straight in the eyes.

"Fred, I know it doesn't make sense to you. But as the company has grown considerably the last couple of years, its leadership needs have changed. With the newest round of venture funding coming into the company, the question is being asked if I'm the right guy to take the company to the next level."

"The right guy? Of course you are. The team loves you, man. And look at the job you've done in guiding the company to where it is today. How could you not be the right guy?" Fred was clearly exasperated.

"Thanks for your vote of confidence, Fred. It means a lot to me. Really, it does. But in some respects, the final decision is out of my hands."

"Well, we have to find some way to keep you with the company, Tim. That's all I have to say."

"Fred, you are passionate about the company—and I really appreciate that. We both want what is best for iCyt and its people. At this point, it's looking like I will be leaving sometime later this year. I promise to do my best in the transition process—and I'll do all I can to remain on the board, cheering the company on to success."

Our dinnertime conversation was over. We got up slowly from our chairs and gave each other a hug.

It's said there are two things certain in this life: death and taxes.

I think there's a third certainty: Things change.

I had been CEO of iCyt for seven-and-a-half good years. Years of struggle and growth, of building teams and achieving goals. We had done the two-step shuffle—two steps forward, one step back—but our overall direction was definitely forward.

But as a young company grows, there are inflection points, turning points where significant change—often affecting a company's leadership —occurs. Typically, the executive skill set that was so essential in getting a start-up to a certain stage is not the same as the one required for the proverbial next level of growth. And there are typically differing opinions on how, why, and when leadership changes should be implemented. The company board members may have one or more views, investors another perspective, and management team members still another.

Such a time came for iCyt in the spring of 2008. We were growing in leaps and bounds. We had a new round of venture funding coming in. We had a hard-working team of researchers and developers who were creating innovative products and a sales and service team that was top notch. We had established a toehold in the competitive landscape that was typically dominated by much larger companies.

And, as CEO, I had the strong and unqualified support of most everyone in the company.

But there were emerging philosophical differences between me and one key member of the Board in how to run the company. Those differences had become very difficult to manage, and ultimately, I couldn't see a way to navigate the troubled waters.

So within a month of returning from Budapest, I announced to the iCyt team that I would be leaving the company. Though I would continue to work in a consulting role until the end of 2008, the plan was to resign as CEO by July 31. I was proud of my tenure there—being part of a team that grew the entity from scratch into one of the leading innovators in our industry with 50 employees and millions in revenue. But it was time for someone else to take the reins and strategize the way forward.

It was a bittersweet moment. Getting relieved of one's duties is certainly one of the most poignant reminders that we're not really in control, no matter the perceived importance of our role or feelings of irreplaceability. It's also a reminder that few situations in life are permanent. We are seasonal residents of our life experiences—and when the seasons change, even those that have lasted for many years, it is best to embrace the change. And so I did—with a certain lightness coming over me by releasing the day-to-day obligations of iCyt and anticipating what might be next.

My final day in the office at iCyt was July 31 of that year. For seven-and-a-half years it had been an exhilarating yet difficult journey. As the company grew, the stakes of the game were raised, and I felt increasingly responsible for the success of our company and the 50 or so families that relied on iCyt for their livelihood. Because we were a high-tech company with a cutting-edge line of products, there was considerable risk in every phase of our business: raising enough capital to continue research and development; establishing a toehold in the competitive landscape dominated by large companies; keeping our team highly focused on our objectives; ensuring that our products performed properly and were serviced well; and keeping the checkbook balanced! There were days that the weight of all that risk quite literally sapped all of my strength. Sleepless nights became the norm in 2007 and 2008, in particular.

So the opportunity to switch gears and do something entirely different was indeed a welcome one, though it came in a manner and time that I didn't quite expect. After announcing my departure from iCyt to the staff, I began to consider a variety of options for the "next thing to do." Re-entering the management consulting industry was attractive to me, with the knowledge and experience I'd gained from running SourceGear and iCyt. But before conceiving and ultimately diving into the launch of my new consulting endeavor, Serra Ventures, I was sensing that it was time for a meaningful break. I decided that the month of August would be a sabbatical from work. During this time, I didn't have a rigid agenda or schedule, and that was actually very liberating. I decided that I would take this time to focus on three things:

- Honey-do projects around the house—paint the fence, fix up the landscape, do some household chores for my number one fan, Toni
- Family time—enjoy the time with our three daughters, including a family vacation to San Diego, before they each returned to school for the fall
- Relationship building—connecting with important people in my life over a cup of coffee or lunch

After 25 years in business, this was the first time I had a significant block of time set aside with nothing scheduled that related to work. The thought was a bit terrifying: In a quarter century, this would be the first time that I would not be working for a month! I was hoping that this time would refresh and energize me. I was seeking new ideas and new insights. I was praying for a time of personal transformation. As I stepped away from and released everyday stresses, I was giving God the opportunity to move in a unique way in my life—to reshape, renew, and revitalize me.

Puttering around in the yard restored a connection to my landscaping roots. I felt blessed to have the time to stop and appreciate the beauty and simplicity of a hibiscus, the stately nature of the swamp white oak, and the whimsy of the river birch. With no "big problems" to solve, I was able to soak up the rejuvenation of just being in the garden. Funny how the creation has so much to tell us, if we'd only slow down enough to really listen to it.

The family time was also special. Our trip to San Diego was one of the most memorable vacations that I can recall. We made the most of visiting old haunts, hitting Coronado Beach, spending a day at Disneyland, picking up treats from our favorite donut place and eating them at Hilltop Park, watching movies together and just "being with." We laughed, told stories, relived old memories, created new ones, and of course, had a few family arguments!

Finally, I seemed to gain new energy from connecting with people close to me throughout the month. I shared a casual cup of coffee or lunch with several folks. The conversations seemed to be following a familiar theme.

"So, what's it like to be out of a job?" my friend, David Hodge, asked.

"It's been pretty refreshing, actually. Lots of family time. Rediscovering my handyman skills. Generally causing havoc in Toni's schedule."

"Sounds like fun. Wish it was me, buddy."

"I suppose everyone should take a month off," I laughed.

"What's next, then?" David's tone was a bit more serious.

"I've been noodling on a lot of different things. The one that keeps resonating with me is to hang the consulting shingle back out again—and maybe create a firm around myself. It feels a little risky though. Doing it before with LifeVision, back in the late '90s, didn't work out so well. What happens if I fall on my face again, man?"

"Yeah, I know what you mean. If you took a different approach this time around, what changes would you make?"

"Well, for starters, I would be much more focused on a particular set of customers versus being all things to all people. I'd focus on serving high technology start-ups. I've learned quite a bit from the last decade or so of leading technology firms, so why not put that to use? Secondly, I would seek out a like-minded team to share my vision of building a full-service firm helping these start-ups get off the ground with business planning, funding help, and strategy development—the whole nine yards."

"You know, Tim, I'm sensing that that is exactly what God has wired you to do," David stated with confidence.

"Really? That's what my brother Ben said just last week. At least the two of you are in agreement!"

David and Ben were confirming what others were saying. As I related different pieces of my vision for this next life chapter to a handful of close friends, I was in turn receiving helpful feedback and encouragement. So, while I was officially "resting" and taking time off during the month of August, I was benefitting from the unexpected bonus of having my vision for Serra Ventures confirmed. I've found that this phenomenon is not unusual—in fact, in the middle of "active rest" is where my most powerful life moments have occurred. It seems that it's in this special place of non-activity, or a different kind of activity, that God speaks. He will confirm a decision I'm pondering; nudge me to consider a new way of thinking on an old problem; or give me insight on reaching out to someone.

By September 1, I was full of enthusiasm and vision for the new thing I would be doing—starting Serra Ventures, a consultancy offering a range of services to the University of Illinois start-up community. In many ways, this was the start of my "third career" and likely the one that would take me to the finish line (first career being professional service provider with McGladrey & Pullen and LifeVision from 1983 to 2000; my second career one of running the tech companies SourceGear and iCyt from 2000 to 2008). Taking the month of August off—finding time to rest and approach life differently—had indeed brought focus, energy, and refreshment. I was ready to hit the ground running.

These many years later, I am embracing full-on the "Serra Ventures" chapter of life. In that short time, I've gained two full-time partners in Dennis Beard and Rob Schultz, while being joined by David Hodge on a part-time basis; added my daughter Alyssa to our team in 2009 as the marketing and communications coordinator; hired my son-in-law Eric in 2013 as a consultant and analyst; provided positions for various interns; launched two venture capital funds to provide seed stage capital to start-ups; provided services to nearly 100 start-ups; and grown our revenue base substantially.

Yet, most of that really feels to me like foundation-laying for what God is about to do next. In some ways, the more substantive part of the Serra Ventures life chapter is just now beginning to take shape. Honestly, this is the most enthused I've been about work in my lifetime. The opportunities on the horizon loom large and exciting. And in many ways what I am experiencing now is due in large part to the restful break of August 2008. The vision and early plans for Serra Ventures came together through the process of active rest, not hands-on, day-to-day work.

Sounds like God to me.

25. The Best Sammich I Ever Had

Champaign, Illinois
March 2013
Vis a vis Waco, Texas
April 2010

I WAS SITTING IN THE CHAMPAIGN JIMMY JOHN'S ON KIRBY AND MATTIS, experiencing an all-out assault on each of my senses. The aroma of fresh-baked bread was probably the most noticeable thing. Mmmmm. Put me in just the right mood to devour the Vito sandwich in front of me (that's the Italian sub, with yummy hot peppers, three different meats, crunchy veggies and Italian dressing). But I was also struck by the strong visual cues around me—bold red, black, and white colors, great graphics, and lots of quirky signage like "Your Mom Wants You to Eat at Jimmy John's" and "We'd Love to See You Naked, But the Health Department Requires Clothes." Throw in exceptional cleanliness, loud rockin' music, a bunch of employees who seem to really be enjoying themselves, and you have the picture of what is making JJ's the third-fastest growing restaurant franchise in the country.

Aside from their delicious, unique sandwiches, I've long admired many facets of the Jimmy John's franchise, having had essentially a front row seat to their amazing growth since being founded in 1983. JJ's started on the campus of Eastern Illinois University in Charleston, Illinois, just 40 miles south of Champaign, my hometown. Today, their largest concentration of company-owned stores is here in Champaign, as is their corporate headquarters.

The Jimmy John's chain now has over 2,000 stores nationwide, and per-store sales averages are well above the industry averages. The JJ's concept is to offer a limited menu and serve all sandwiches cold and in less than 30 seconds! With an emphasis on quality, lightning-fast execution, and delivery service, it is no wonder that JJ's is an industry leader.

Our three daughters had plenty of exposure to JJ's while growing up in Champaign. Audra, our middle child, was what I affectionately call the "Jimmy John's freak" of the family. I think she could eat a JJ sandwich pretty much every day of the week. So when Audra went off to Baylor University in 2007, it was the start of several years of pining and complaining about why there was no Jimmy John's in Waco, Texas. While visiting Audra during spring break of 2010, I was listening to the 65th or so complaint of her hankering for JJ's. So, I went on to their website, did a little poking around, and discovered that McClennan County, Texas, was open for franchising. I was a little surprised, to be honest; Jimmy John's had over 50 restaurants throughout the state of Texas at that time, and I figured that surely someone would have snatched up the Waco market. I zipped off an email to their Director of Franchising, Bob Morena, and got a response within a few hours—yes, Waco was available, and I was welcome to apply for a franchise there. Strange how quickly this lark of an idea seemed to be gaining momentum. I stopped to pray, "God, if this opportunity is of you, give me confirmation to proceed. I invite you to lead me and give me wisdom. And, I ask you to shut this deal down if it doesn't fit into your bigger scheme for my life."

Sensing no stop signs from above, rather a growing sense of this being the right thing, my next step was picking up the phone to call my business partners in Gameday Spirit, Steve Vogelsang and David Hodge. I knew that this opportunity would take a team to pull off—and the three of us were already doing something similar with Gameday.

"Hey guys, thanks for getting on a conference call at last minute notice. Appreciate it."

"No problem, Tim. What's up?" David asked.

"I know this is going to sound crazy—maybe completely out of left field—but what do you guys think about Jimmy John's?" I asked.

"I love the Pepe sandwich the best," Steve said, "but I suspect that's not what you're asking."

I laughed. "Right, Steve. I'm thinking, what if we put together a franchisee group and opened some Jimmy John's stores in Waco, Texas? Would you guys be interested in joining me?"

"Sounds intriguing," David said. But I can think of a lot of reasons why this also sounds a little crazy. Like, how do we practically execute this idea, seeing as we all live about nine hundred miles from Waco?"

"David, that is one very good question, along with fifteen others that I can think of. I really have no idea how we can pull this off, but the Waco market is available—and I sense we've got to move pretty quickly if we're interested in this. I've got a meeting set up with Bob Morena next week at the JJ headquarters in Champaign. If y'all can join me, we can start gathering the information we need to make a decision."

David and Steve said they were willing to take that next step, and with that, we were off to the races. A meeting with Bob took place that following week—and our headlong tumble toward becoming franchisees had begun. In addition to Steve and David, I asked Dennis (my partner in Serra Ventures) if he would like to join the team. He agreed. It all seemed to be falling into place. The opportunity was ours for the taking. The team was in place. The capital to open a couple of stores was available. God was green-lighting this deal.

Or, was he? After a few weeks of sheer exhilaration and excitement, I began to be gripped—is paralyzed too strong a word here?—with the reality of just how difficult it would be to start and operate a franchise business located in Waco, Texas, a city and state we really knew nothing about from a business perspective. Our partners each had day jobs—in fact, we all were involved in at least two businesses and a variety of nonwork activities to boot. Would we have enough time to devote to this new enterprise? Was the risk level acceptable? What if we failed? The questions were beginning to mount and a wave of doubt was washing over me. By the beginning of April, I was beginning to think we were making a big mistake.

Like many significant decisions in my past, this decision had the strong sense of being a "God thing." Meaning, it fit into the bigger scheme of my life purpose, and that of my business colleagues, and was in alignment with God's bigger story of setting things right in the world. This business opportunity had the potential for impact in a variety of arenas—economic, relational, and spiritual—and the vision for it had captured me initially. But, now a few weeks in, I wasn't so sure. The questions inside my head were screaming at me. How were we going to find a team in Waco to operate the stores? How were we going to do site selection from 900 miles away? Were we prepared for the inevitable glitches that would occur? How many trips to Waco would be required to make sure that the business was getting off the ground and operating well? What would happen if we fell flat on our face and lost our significant investment? The questions and doubt had me looking for a way out of this crazy decision!

In mid-April, I made a follow-up trip to Waco. While there, I received a call from Bob Morena. He asked about our progress, and I gave him an edited update. Looking for a potential way out, I asked Bob, "Has any other Texas franchisee called to ask about the Waco market?" I was hoping he would say yes, that they could possibly award the Waco market to someone else, and that they would in the end, graciously let us off the hook. Interestingly, he did say that another franchisee had called and asked about Waco, but that he told the caller our group had been selected with confidence. Well, so much for having JJ corporate let us off the hook.

With a real sense of unease, I went about the rest of the weekend looking for some kind of evidence or a sign that this business deal was going to work. On Sunday, I attended services at Antioch Community Church, where Audra and Kaley attended. The head pastor, named Jimmy Siebert (everything seemed to be coming up "Jimmy" those days!), had been presenting a short sermon series on Living Simply, Working Diligently, and Giving Generously over the previous weeks.

The topic for that particular Sunday was giving generously. Jimmy's message was stirring and authentic to the core. I could tell that this was something he had lived deeply and with conviction for many years. During the message, I had this strange sense come over me that something powerful was about to happen. And, indeed, the 20 minutes that followed Jimmy's sermon were one of the most poignant "power encounters" of my life.

At the end of the service, Jimmy invited everyone that was struggling with finances to the stage area for prayer and then invited up the Antioch prayer team. The response from people desiring prayer was so overwhelming that Jimmy issued a blanket call for anyone who had experience praying for others to come up front and assist. He then issued a very strange directive, unlike I've ever heard prior or since. "If you're here to help pray, as God directs you, take a ten or twenty from your wallet and give it to the person you're praying for—as a small sign to that person that God will provide." My good friend Greg Leman looked at me with a smile, grabbed my arm, and we both proceeded to the stage area where dozens and dozens of people were awaiting prayer. What unfolded over the next several minutes was one of the most joyous, weird, beautiful, crazy things I have ever been part of. Nearly a couple hundred people were now gathered in the stage area—some praying, others receiving prayer, some crying, others bent down on their knees, some with their hands raised, and others in quiet wonderment as the Spirit's wind moved over the crowd. Prayers were prayed, and cash was being pulled out of wallets and given right then and there to those in need; still others were getting out of their seats to bring cash to Jimmy so that he in turn could hand it off to someone being prayed for.

The first man I encountered said he was out of work and he was seeking God's provision for a job so he could provide for his wife and two kids. Tears were falling down his cheeks as he quietly shared his heart with me. Unable to hold back tears myself, I placed my hands on his shoulders and was overcome with God's compassion for this 30-something man desperate for help. Managing a few feeble words of prayer, I then pulled $40 out of my wallet and folded it into his hands.

In that singular moment, I heard God's Spirit speak to me, "This is why you have been given the opportunity to build a business in Waco."

My heart broke as I received a fresh revelation of God's heart for people—that he cares about each of our most basic needs. And so it was at that moment that I realized that Jimmy John's in Waco was, at its foundation, about providing jobs—perhaps one of the most fundamental elements of God's kingdom taking root in someone's life. If we accomplished nothing other than providing jobs by opening stores in Waco, we were doing something meaningful and significant in God's bigger scheme. In rereading my personal journal from that day, here is what I wrote: "I have been encouraged to move forward and meet the challenges of executing on this plan—of which I am sure there will be plenty. God is giving us an awesome opportunity to partner with him in this— may he also give us tremendous grace to get the job done!"

Shortly after that weekend, we interviewed and hired Larry Wright to be the general manager and leader of our team in Waco. Interestingly, Larry was attending Antioch and had previously served with his family as a missionary in Brazil. Larry (supported by his wife Kristie) has been a key ingredient, and the real difference-maker, in leading our on-the-ground team in Waco. He has spearheaded our efforts to open six stores, with more on the way. He has been the main cog in the machine that is now providing over 150 jobs in Waco, many of them supervisory and managerial in nature.

And while I have been proud of cooperating with God to provide jobs, the process of developing our Jimmy John's business has been anything but easy. My faith and resolve have been tested numerous times over the last four years with construction challenges and cost overruns, significant personnel issues including turnover and employee drug use, banking woes that centered around a protracted six months of renegotiating our loan structure, and struggles to become profitable. In fact, it has taken us four years to stabilize the company and consistently earn a profit. Remaining resilient in the face of setbacks and failures has been tough.

But on a recent visit there, I was reminded that this business endeavor really is in bigger hands than my own.

"I never thought I would have an opportunity like this," Kelly (not her real name) said in a gathering of our managers and assistant managers.

"What do you mean, Kelly?" I asked.

"Well, I'm a single mother who has experienced a lot of difficulty in the last ten years. At times, I thought life would be one big dead-end for me. I started as a line worker here a year ago or so—and now I'm an assistant manager. I just want to keep growing and moving up here at Jimmy John's," she said. I could hear the pride in her voice and see a glint in her eye.

That was a touching moment—and one that solidified for me that we are on the right path as a business, regardless of the ups and downs we've experienced. We're doing our best to cooperate with the Holy Spirit in building a solid business based on kingdom values. There will be more challenges, I'm sure. But just as with the difficulties of the past few years, I can anchor my thoughts and perspective in the "power encounter" at Antioch Community Church in April 2010, and move forward with a clear resolve that this was and is about something bigger than ourselves.

PART 3

Relationships

L ife is an amazing journey. And it's best experienced with others. God intended it this way, to be in community with each other. This section explores the meaningfulness, the power and the blessing of "doing life together." .

26. You Reap What You Sow

Normal, Illinois
August 2003

IT WAS MOVE-IN DAY AT ILLINOIS STATE UNIVERSITY, August 21, 2003. Students, parents, friends, and family were scrambling up and down stairs, sweating profusely, staring confusedly at the small spaces in front of them—with the goal of fitting in ALL that stuff! Thousands of students trying to move into one building in a period of four to six hours, a building 20 floors tall, with elevators that stopped every fifth floor (you get to walk up or down at least two flights of stairs to finish your journey—now, who thought of that idea?). When we did manage to get the 25 loads of stuff up to our daughter's room, at first glance it seemed impossible to fit everything in. Then we realized that only half of the room was hers. Alyssa's roommate was coming up right behind her!

A majority of college campuses still house students in dorms constructed in the '50s, '60s, and '70s, back when students brought to school a typewriter, an alarm clock, some clothing, and a picture or two. Today's college students bring stereos, microwaves, computers, iPads, refrigerators, printers, furniture, and televisions (and quite a few more clothes, if our three daughters are a statistically valid sample). This is a formula for a pretty crowded scenario in most dorm rooms. Enter bedloft.com, a company created to address the problem of dorm rooms' limited space.

Bedloft.com offers a simple loft product that lofts the existing dorm room bed five feet to create instant living space beneath. The company works through exclusive arrangements with a university's housing department. Students rent the loft for the school year through an online portal, the university housing department receives a modest commission, and bedloft.com delivers the lofts! It's a win-win-win! This company now serves over 80 colleges and universities throughout the U.S. and is led by Ryan Majeres. Ryan is a University of Illinois grad who knows how to work hard, has a nose for business, and is focused on delivering solutions to his customers.

I first met Ryan in 2001 at the Vineyard Church in Urbana. I don't recall exactly how we were introduced to each other, but I do remember being quite impressed in our first couple of lunches together. In one of those early conversations, over sandwiches at Biaggi's, Ryan shared his desire to one day own his own business.

"I am burning the candle at both ends, Tim. Yes, I'm having success, but I wish all of this effort was building equity for me and my family."

"Understood. Guys like you—who are laying it all out there and doing really well helping a business grow—often want an opportunity to build a business for themselves," I empathized. "You'll get your chance."

"Do you think so? Some days I wonder," Ryan said as he took a bite of his Italian beef.

"Yes, I do, Ryan. Keep working hard—and keep your eyes and ears open for opportunity. One of these days, I'm thinking soon, you'll have that opportunity to be an entrepreneur."

"The owner of the company I'm working for has thrown out some hints about selling the company. I wonder if he'd consider me a potential buyer?" Ryan said.

"Perhaps. It's pretty common, in fact, for buyers of companies to have some prior relationship with the seller. You'd be a good bet in my book."

Ryan sat back and gave me a rueful grin. "Just a couple of small problems, Tim. One, I've never run a business before, and two, I have no cash to buy the business."

"Well, the first one I can help you with. I can come alongside and guide you through the process, if you're open to it. The second one is a bit trickier—but I think we can solve that one, too."

Ryan and I continued to meet over the course of three years, probably two to three times a year. He would give me the update from his road warrior episodes, with the conversation typically turning to his frustration about working hard but not building any equity, and about his continuing dream of owning a company one day. Basically, we revisited our Biaggi's conversation, with new developments thrown in every now and then. Although I was "in the business" of offering my advice for a fee, I decided that this was a relationship worth investing in—at no charge. I honestly didn't expect to profit monetarily, but I was enjoying the satisfaction of seeing a young person grapple with the growing dream in his heart. Over the years, I've encountered many more young people like Ryan who are presently employed but have a vision for becoming an entrepreneur. It's one of the real joys I get to experience: seeing people work out their vision over time and ultimately having the opportunity to realize those dreams!

With Ryan, I did my best to encourage him to keep the dream alive, reinforcing my earlier words to him that he would get the opportunity at the right time. I also encouraged him with the perspective that from my vantage point, he possessed all of the ingredients to be a successful entrepreneur. Although he was frustrated in his work circumstances, I told him it was great preparation for the future, and he should view his present difficulty in that light. Easy to say. Tough to embrace.

Interestingly, I was experiencing my own set of frustrations with regard to entrepreneurship during those three years of meeting with Ryan. Having failed with LifeVision and moved on from SourceGear, I wasn't seeing a lot of evidence that the things I was sharing with Ryan really worked. Yet the advice I offered to Ryan still made sense to me and was something in which I deeply believed. I knew in my heart that the thoughts I shared with Ryan were indeed essential to achieving success in an entrepreneurial endeavor—regardless of my own frustrations at the time.

In essence, my encouragement to Ryan was a series of statements made in faith as opposed to grounded in my own reality. These encouragements were mirrored in an article I read many years later, titled "10 Characteristics of Superior Leaders" (Dr. David Javitch, Entrepreneur Magazine, Dec 9, 2009). Dr. Javitch's work found that successful entrepreneurs had a clear mission, vision, and goals, which are things I have always believed to be essential to a business leader. Among other characteristics were perseverance, strong interpersonal skills, a "get it done attitude," and a combination of ambition and inspiration. I saw all of these characteristics in Ryan, and I was determined to see him succeed. I could sense that Ryan had a strong desire to step out, take a risk, and make a difference—and that he was driven by a God-given inspiration to be a business owner, a creator of opportunity both for himself and others.

In late 2003, the owner of Ryan's company did indeed come to him with an offer to sell Ryan the business. That's when Ryan and my relationship changed from casual, two or three times a year lunch pals, to full-fledged business partners. Ryan asked if I would come along side of him to get the purchase of the business done and to help launch the new company, bedloft.com. Although he felt confident in his skills to run the business day to day, he needed help to get the transaction completed and to set a large-scale strategy for the company's growth. Needless to say, it was an exciting opportunity that fit well with my experience and skills, and sounded like fun! We worked out an arrangement where Ryan would be majority owner of the new company, and I would take a minority stock position in the company in return for my efforts as his business partner.

The next six months were full of the typical ups and downs of "doing a deal"—that is, one day the deal was on, and the next it would be off; the seller would make a certain set of statements and demands, and we would counter them; we would sail from one big high to a devastating low. In my experience, most purchase/sale transactions go like this, frustrating as it is. However, In July of 2004, we got the deal done! Collegiate Marketing, Inc., doing business as bedloft.com, was born! The company started off with about 22 customers, mostly colleges in the Midwest.

Ryan has worked hard to build the company into its present form (with me helping mostly from the sidelines, in the role of coach and cheerleader). The company has over 80 college accounts today and many times the revenue as when we purchased the company so many years ago. But while the business growth and financial success are gratifying, I'm most encouraged by the tremendous growth I've seen in Ryan—a person who went from hardworking employee to business owner, visionary, and a creator of good-paying jobs, a prime example of what small businesses are providing for the people of this country. I'm blessed to have seen my personal relationship with him grow into a business partnership and equally thrilled that Ryan has gone way beyond what he'd originally hoped for or imagined.

27. Breaking Up Is Hard to Do

Champaign, Illinois
November 2004

JOHN CHISHOLM AND I GO WAY BACK. So do lots of close friends. But our relationship was different, deeper, more connected than most.

John was my small group pastor in the late 1980s and early 1990s. We met regularly to discuss a wide range of topics, usually at the Olive Garden (unlimited soup, salad, and breadsticks!), becoming quite fond of one another in those initial years of our relationship.

John was the mission team leader on the 1992 trip to the Czech Republic on which I was a team member (see Chapter 13). A critical interaction with him on that trip became the catalyst for me in wrestling with the topic of personal purpose, role alignment, and my personal vision for the future. It led to a 20-year adventure with these important topics, and in a sense, was the starting point for this book.

John worked as an advisor to my team of consultants at McGladrey in 1993, with the goal of developing our interpersonal skills, specifically conflict resolution and team communication. By that time, he had left the pastorate and formed a company called North Star Strategies, specializing in assisting teams at churches and businesses with teamwork and communication issues. Bringing John in to work with our team led to great success—and it seemed that he was one of us by the time we'd worked together for a year.

John came to California to work with an important client of mine in 1996. To a complex situation, he brought his masterful brand of retreat facilitation—wowing the client in exceptional ways. (By the end of that retreat, they really did like him better than me!)

John and I joined forces as official cofounders and partners in a new consulting company called LifeVision, Inc. in 1998. We figured we'd done so much life together in 10 years, why not go into business with each other?

John and I each bought one third of Gameday Spirit from Steve Vogelsang in late 1999. LifeVision had been engaged to help Steve sell the company—and when that didn't work, we did the next best thing: John and I each bought a piece of Gameday, forming a three-way partnership that led to years of enjoyment (and profits!).

John joined with me at iCyt in 2002 to play a key role in helping the company launch the sales effort for our new laser device, the Lyt. We faced numerous challenges, but John had worked as a jewelry salesman in the 1980s, developing key sales skills and expertise, and he confidently went about building a successful sales system and team for iCyt.

You might say that John and I were connected seven ways to Sunday. Business colleagues. Co-workers. Partners. Intimate associates. Best friends.

John appeared in the doorway to my iCyt office that mid-November day in 2004 with an unusual, somewhat pained look on his face.

"Tim, if you and Steve have time for lunch this Thursday, there's something important I'd like to discuss with both of you," John said in a subdued, uncharacteristic tone. Pained look. Strange voice inflection. Something was up.

"Sure, Chiz. How about Olive Garden? Haven't been there in a while."

"That works. See if Vogie is available, will you?"

I picked up the phone to see if Thursday would work for Steve, too. It did. We were all set. In two days, we all met at the Olive Garden out by Marketplace Mall in Champaign.

"Thanks, guys, for getting together today," John said in a matter-of-fact tone. "Let me get right to the point. I've decided that it's time for me to break away from Gameday, and I'd like the two of you to consider buying me out."

"Really, Chiz? Are you joking?" I asked, quite seriously. I hadn't expected this. A problem or two to work through, possibly—but not this.

"I'm not joking. There's a lot that's happened over the last couple of years. I believe that in important ways, we've grown apart and are no longer on the same page, particularly in a spiritual sense. I've reviewed our buy-sell agreement. I have a price in mind that I'd like you to pay, and I believe it's fair. I'd appreciate it if we didn't have to negotiate."

I was perplexed. Steve, too. I could see it written all over his face. Dumbfounded was perhaps the better choice of words for us both. John was an Illinois alum (Gameday sells licensed Illinois sportswear and gifts). John was a sports nut—a high school basketball star that seemed to get better with age. In college, John ran the "student card section" at football games and his then girlfriend, now wife, Fran, played in the Fighting Illini Marching Band. John had a passion for Illinois sports that was more rabid than most; he really did bleed orange and blue.

Further, John was not only a financial investor in Gameday, but he had become its driving force. He pushed our management team, our employees, and Steve and me to make the business the best it could be. He was Gameday. So it was an understatement to say that Gameday had been the perfect fit for John. That was prima facie. Done. No argument. In the bank. So where was this idea of being bought out coming from?

As the three of us processed over lunch, emotions ran high. Appetites were lost. Very difficult words were exchanged. My take was that John's request to separate from Steve and me basically boiled down to some deeply-held theological beliefs that had been incubating for several years inside him. Those beliefs were beginning to manifest in some pretty major action steps for John—and selling Gameday was one of the biggest pieces of this theological puzzle. In short, John considered himself out of alignment with Steve and me regarding the mission, vision, and values of Gameday.

The distraught look on Steve's face as he wrestled with John's explanation of "why" told me just how deeply offended he was. I, too, was struggling with a growing sense of disbelief and confusion. It's common, I suppose, to feel personally rejected in a situation like this—and nobody likes that. Clearly, this had caught Steve and me off-guard. I stumbled over my words, trying to form some sense of reasonable objection. That was the only response I could drum up that made sense.

"The Illini have a chance to be really special this year," I offered.

"I know that, Tim. Could be Final Four bound, for all we know," John replied.

"So, it doesn't seem rational to buy you out now, John. Why not see how the season plays out? It's only November, my friend. Maybe Dee Brown and Deron Williams will do what no other Illinois basketball team has done—carry us to the national title."

"I love Deron and Dee—Luther and Roger, too. They are a special team. But, no, my decision is my decision. It's time to get a deal done."

The cold reality of what was going down began to grip me. Our grand adventure of doing "Gameday life together" as three partners and indeed, three couples (our wives really liked each other) seemed inevitably headed for the relational dumpster, and soon. For me, though, the ramifications were even deeper than the cessation of the Gameday partnership—what would this mean to all of the other ways in which John and I were connected?

Chiz, as his close friends called him, and I met in 1989 when he moved his family to Champaign to accept an unpaid position at the Vineyard Church. Chiz had been a very successful sales career in the Chicago area, but he'd hit a spiritual wall of frustration that ultimately brought him south to Illini country. He was intrigued by the health and vitality of the Vineyard Church in Champaign, and both he and Fran believed that it was the right move for their growing family, despite the lack of a job, few relational connections, and a number of other unknowns. Suffice it to say they took a very bold risk moving south.

John became the volunteer extraordinaire, working whenever and in whatever role he was assigned. His work ethic, his passion, and his trustworthiness did not go unnoticed. He was offered a church staff position overseeing small group leaders within the year. Because of his new role, and mine as a small group leader, John and I soon began a relationship that ultimately became one of the most rich and satisfying friendships of my life.

Soon after the fateful lunch meeting, the unraveling of our relationship accelerated. Not only was a departure from Gameday on the table, but over the next two to three weeks, we were talking about John's departure from iCyt and from our (somewhat dormant) consulting company, LifeVision. Early in January, I thought I'd take one more crack at salvaging things.

"Are you sure you want to proceed with this, Chiz?" I asked, leaning against the doorframe of his office at iCyt.

"I know this is hard to accept, Tim, but yes, I do."

"Well, our b-ball team has been ranked number one in the country for several weeks now. Like I said at the lunch in November, why not wait and see how this basketball season ends. You could be walking away from a tremendous financial boon—only weeks away. If Illinois proceeds to go as far as we all think in the NCAA tourney, the fan response will be incredible for Gameday," I said.

"Yes, I know that. It's a risk I'm willing to take. "

"And are you sure we should also buy you out of iCyt and LifeVision? Do you really want to do those deals, as well?"

"Makes sense to do them all at the same time, Tim."

It would become a trifecta of business separations happening in record time. Indeed, by February 2005, John had been bought out of his positions in Gameday, iCyt, and LifeVision. We'd been able to draw up the paperwork rather quickly—and though there were some significant issues to work through (think price and terms for three businesses!), we did get the issues resolved without getting into any fistfights.

With the signing of the sale documents, a rawness of emotion overwhelmed me. John handed me the last page of the sale agreement, I placed it the manila folder and closed it, and placed the folder in front of me on the attorney's conference room table. John smiled, pushed his chair back, rose, and said goodbye. I sat alone in the room with my thoughts. And began to quietly cry.

With the ink barely dry on the sale agreements, John and I ceased to communicate on pretty much all levels. Business. Life. Family. Our intimate, nearly day-to-day interaction—which had been a staple in both of our lives for over 15 years—was over. I suppose the blame for that was shared by both of us. It was quite awkward from that point forward, and there wasn't much of a practical reason to be talking much. For me, the pain was very real—and the pain felt heightened by what had been the suddenness, the completeness, the finality of the separation. Additional salt in the wound seemed to stem from the very business-like, transactional nature of what went down. It didn't feel like the right way to say goodbye. I reached out to those closest to me to process and make sense of it.

"I'm not sure how to describe it, Toni, but this feels like a divorce to me. Not that you or I have been through that—but this is what it must feel like," I said.

"I think you're right, honey. I can see the pain in your eyes and in your body language."

"You mean it's that obvious? Rats. I was hoping to fool a few folks." I was only half-serious.

"You and John were dear friends, brothers in every sense of the word. So to separate like this is every bit as painful as a divorce of spouses, I'm sure." Toni touched my shoulder and gave me a peck on the lips.

"Well I just don't understand it, and that's the hardest part."

Although the processing with Toni and others did help, I continued to feel empty, deeply hurt, and confused for months. There was little about the breakdown of our relationship that I really understood. I had a handle on certain reasons behind it, but was never able to fully comprehend it.

About a year later, John reached out to me and we scheduled a lunch.

"I want to say I'm sorry for how the whole deal went down between us, Tim. Will you forgive me?" John asked.

"Of course, Chiz. That's the least I can do. I'm still hurt; perhaps you are too. I don't suppose either of us can undo that. Will you forgive me for the things I said and did in the process?"

"Yes, I will. But you're right, I don't think we can ever undo what was done."

"Well, I want to bless you and the new direction you've taken. I want God's best for you."

"Thanks, Tim. I really appreciate that. Only time will tell how these decisions will work out."

Over the eight years since that conversation, John and I have met periodically to get caught up on one another's lives. I think we'd both agree that it hasn't been the same as it was those first 15 years of being in regular relationship with each other. Too many dramatic shifts have occurred. But I think we've both been able to move on and heal, and we both genuinely want the best for the other.

Some things in life are this way. The "why" of certain events, particularly in relationships, remains unknowable and mysterious. We are complex beings and our behaviors and choices will at times defy simplistic explanations. I am now in a place of celebrating the joy that John and I did share for so many years and the way he shaped my past. I'm a better person for having known him.

28. Sail On

Champaign, Illinois
July 2010

JUSTIN ELKOW AND I FIRST MET EACH OTHER IN A CLASS I WAS TEACHING at the Vineyard Church in Urbana back in 2000. I remember being impressed that this young man would invest time to take a class on a Sunday afternoon when he already had plenty of rigorous academic commitments staring him down. He wasn't just attending the class—he was actively engaged, asking questions, offering comments.

At the end of the class, I learned that Justin was enrolled as a freshman at the University of Illinois in electrical engineering, a program that is consistently ranked among the top five electrical engineering programs worldwide. Most engineering students wouldn't find their way into a bible class on a weekend. For that reason, I took to Justin quite easily. As I began to get to know him, I found Justin to be curious, inquisitive, fun-loving, and—in good alignment with my own interests—eager to learn about entrepreneurship. Over his undergraduate years, we did lunch every now and then. I recall one of our conversations in early 2002.

"How are things for you on campus, Justin?"

"Let's just say that there aren't many dull moments in the life of an engineering student. The professors certainly know how to pile on the projects."

"That's what you get for enrolling in a program that most reasonable human beings have the good sense to stay away from!"

"True. But your plate always seems pretty full too, Tim. How do you manage the variety of businesses you're involved with?"

"Point well taken. I think I was created to be an idea guy and a multitasker. I'm happiest when there are new problems to solve, new products to bring to market, and more giants to be slain."

"Well, I think that's how I'm wired too," Justin said. "Although I'm excited to be earning an engineering degree, I think that's just one piece of what I'm really supposed to do in life. My full aspiration is to use my engineering and problem-solving skills in a business I own."

"Really? That's very cool to hear. Recognizing your 'entrepreneurial calling' early on isn't always easy nor is it common. I encourage you to use that realization to your benefit."

"How so?"

"Because you've recognized a desire to own a business at this early stage of your life, you can begin exploring the principles and tools of entrepreneurship now. For example, the university offers a variety of entrepreneurship courses, workshops, and events. I encourage you to look into those."

And Justin did just that. He took courses in entrepreneurship, attended special workshops on campus and in the Research Park, and continued to pick my brain on the ins and outs of the business world. By the time Justin was in graduate school, iCyt had the opportunity to bring him on board as an engineering intern. Though I didn't directly supervise him, our engineering group was always complimentary of his work and effort. He was a natural engineer, if there is such a thing.

Justin graduated with his master's degree in 2006 and took a job with Intel Corporation in California. Along the way, he married his college sweetheart, Jessica. Although Justin and I didn't see as much of each other after that, we did manage to stay in touch via email. And Justin made periodic visits back to the Midwest to visit family. During those trips, he would usually make it a point to stop by in Champaign for a lunch. Those conversations almost always centered on entrepreneurial topics of one stripe or another.

In short order, Justin decided to dip his toe into the entrepreneurial waters buying some rental property in Champaign-Urbana. That was no small risk, considering he was now a California resident. Indeed, Justin got to experience firsthand the joys of absentee ownership! The emails we exchanged on the topic of being a real estate mogul (tongue firmly in cheek) always brought a wry smile to my face. While one of his real estate investments worked out okay, he got caught in the down cycle of the late 2000s, eventually selling two condos at a significant loss. When I learned about this disappointment, I felt badly for him, but I knew it would pay dividends for Justin along the entrepreneurial pathway. Failure and challenge are typical ingredients in the life stew that leads to later success. If we can examine our failures, learn from them, and have the resolve to stay in the game, we will make better choices and take more informed risks down the road.

So, when Justin showed up in my office in the summer of 2010 with a prototype of an Apple iPad accessory and an idea for starting a new company, I was all ears. I knew he had the entrepreneurial bug, was committed to hard work, and had a bit of failure in his recent past. These were essential to making a new endeavor a success.

Joining Justin and me in the conversation was my business partner Dennis Beard and Justin's business partner Robb Hughes (whom Justin had become good friends with at the University of Illinois).

"The idea I've come up with is a free-standing 'picture frame' that holds an iPad. It simultaneously charges the iPad while acting as a display station," Justin explained, taking the prototype of the device out of the box.

"The market for iPads is definitely exploding—so it makes sense that an accessory like this should do well," I said as I picked up the slick-looking piece of metal and carefully examined it.

"Exactly what we're thinking, Tim. Between my engineering background and Robb's accounting expertise, we have some of the basic ingredients for business success."

"But what you lack is some real business expertise and capital—and that's where we come in, right?" I asked.

"Bingo. You must be reading our minds," Justin chuckled.

Now, putting an engineer with an accountant in a start-up company is a little dangerous, but Dennis and I were intrigued as we heard their pitch. As they related the story of their new venture, Striped Sail, Robb and Justin talked about a vision to create a virtual company that would outsource nearly every key function. I had never worked with a company with this type of business model before. Accounting, engineering design, manufacturing, distribution, PR, and marketing—all would be outsourced. Justin and Robb would focus on being creative forces to come up with new product ideas and then use their virtual connections to execute the ideas quickly.

Dennis, Alyssa, and I (the Serra Ventures team at the time) liked their idea, and liked their initial product. But most importantly, we had faith that this was the right team to make the idea a reality. As with most venture-funding decisions, this one ultimately came down to a strong belief that the key people behind the idea could pull it off. I knew that Justin and Robb would have the attitude to "do whatever it takes" in hopes of making the company a success. As we considered the potential upside, while being fully aware of the multiple challenges faced by all start-up companies, we came to a decision. This was a deal that was worth the risk.

From the very beginning, Striped Sail had so many things going for it—a neat product, a talented team, venture funding—but the market did not embrace the offering. And at the end of the day, unless customers embrace your product and vote with their wallets, nothing else really matters. So three years later, Justin, Robb, and Serra Ventures had to make the difficult decision to shut the business down. It was a wrenching moment for all of us.

In its very brief lifetime, the company ran into one significant challenge after another. Manufacturing abroad, while it sounds appealing and cost-saving in theory, had a very unique set of difficulties associated with it. Likewise, selling an accessory to an Apple product meant we had to roll with the punches of a very large corporation calling the shots.

For example, just after getting our initial iPad accessory manufacturing run completed, Apple announced the introduction of the iPad II—and of course, its dimensions and overall form factor had changed just enough to make the Striped Sail product obsolete. The company also missed a 2010 Christmas introduction of the product, experienced rising per-unit cost estimates, and ran into the gale force winds of getting social media coverage amidst a lot of noise in the Apple accessories marketplace.

And while I am disappointed about shutting down the company and losing our venture fund's investment, I am encouraged and upbeat about the future of Robb and Justin as entrepreneurs. They have learned a ton of lessons. The battle scars are pretty fresh—but these guys met nearly every setback with a positive attitude and a passion and commitment to take the right steps towards success. Which is why I'll be all ears when Justin brings me his next idea for a new company.

It truly is fascinating to me that a relationship that started over 15 years ago in a church class has blossomed into what it is today. I feel blessed to have the privilege of adding my business expertise and capital to companies like Striped Sail. More importantly, though, I'm grateful for the opportunity to work with young folks like Justin and Robb. Women and men who have a sincere desire to make the world a better place by bringing novel ideas to fruition—and are willing to take the risks to do so.

As this story illustrates, the outcome isn't guaranteed to be successful. In fact, many new business endeavors will fail. In the case of Justin and Robb, I believe that the best part of the "larger story" is yet to be written. Just like watching a live sporting event, I don't know the outcome, but I'm betting that these two men will "sail on" toward success!

29. A Day (20 Years, Actually) at the Beach

Pentwater, Michigan
July 2010

OUR SMALL CARAVAN OF CARS HAD SNAKED ITS WAY UP BEACH ROAD, reaching the top of what was essentially a massive sand dune covered with fairly dense foliage and brush (and plenty of mosquitoes). The small lamplight on the McVoy Cottage welcomed us, casting a yellowish glow on the makeshift parking lot and the potted impatiens adorning the flagstone landing leading up to the front door. It was about midnight. Our extended family had arrived for what would be the 20th—and final—visit to the lakeside village of Pentwater. What had become an entrenched "Jim Hoerr Family Vacation" tradition was about to do its swan song. One final week of completely restful lollygagging. One final tip of the cap to two decades of hanging with dozens of family members. One more week of priceless memory-building.

Hoops and hollers could be heard throughout the house that night, amidst the unpacking of supplies and hauling of suitcases up the stairs. I took a moment to step on to the outside porch area near the rear of the house. The muffled crash of waves against the shore was magical that night—really, a cadence that evoked a rich flood of memories from our years of gathering in that special place. Like a DVD player in my mind, several scenes of "Pentwaters Past" swept over me.

Scene one: The sun had just dipped below the horizon, darkening the gently lapping waves of Lake Michigan. The June sky was streaked with oranges, purples, and reds—a masterpiece unmatched by human artists. The sweet smell of the campfire smoke was in the air as we settled in around the crackling logs expertly placed by my brother-in-law, Hap. It was "couples night" at the beach, and we were enjoying some time away from our kids, sipping some wine and telling stories. The mood was quite romantic, actually—in a family sort of way. But the mood was rudely disrupted when Mick McCoy, a beach neighbor, crashed the party. He planted himself next to Hap.

I looked at Nancy and Ben, then Joyce. Disappointment was on their faces. This wasn't the plan—and just like that, couples night disintegrated into Mick regaling us with decidedly uninteresting details of his week. Joyce and John were the first to stand up and declare that it was getting late (it was only 8:30 p.m.!). Ben and Tina followed closely behind. And the rest of us followed in short order, one by one heading up to the beach house for the balance of the evening (leaving Hap and Mick to entertain each other). Oh well, so much for a romantic interlude on the beach! In fairness to Mick, I don't think he had a clue what was really going on. And in retrospect, it did end up as one of our more memorable family vacation experiences at Pentwater, Michigan—for all the wrong reasons!

Scene two: The Jim Hoerr extended family was enjoying an evening of board games, including a group playing Scrabble, some engaged in Rummikub, the teens playing a crazy card game called Mafia, and young 'uns immersed in Connect Four. The generous "great room" of the McVoy Cottage, reminiscent of another era, was the perfectly cozy environment for "game night." That is, until one of the young girls—Julie, I think—let out an ear-piercing shriek.

"Eeeeek! A bat!"

"A what? You can't be serious!" Joyce screamed back.

"A bat! I'm not kidding. There is a bat hanging from the ceiling right there."

"No way. What a minute—you're right."

A scream-fest began! Somehow, a bat had found its way into the cottage and proceeded to create havoc. It was soon flitting about, obviously disoriented, causing a good deal of mayhem. Mac, my brother-in-law at the time, became the appointed bat catcher. Armed with a bowl and a stick, Mac and a band of helpers chased the bat throughout the house (multiple rooms involved), until he cornered the poor thing, put the bowl over it, and managed to safely remove the bat from the premises. Problem solved. Hooray, everyone shouted. Instant memory created!

Scene three: I was assigned to the evening dinner crew, with the featured menu item being Tim's not-so-famous marinated chicken, complemented by Crazy Jane baked potatoes, homemade cole slaw, and a nice array of summer fruit. My kitchen crew was a lively, spirited group—my sister, Nancy, one of my kids (Audra), a couple of nieces and nephews. This was the way we did each evening during our annual trip to the beaches of Pentwater—a special menu for each night, an assigned cooking crew, lots of laughter, and quite a few mishaps (10-year-olds make very entertaining kitchen help!). That night in particular, I was in my element. The grill was fired up, and we had a family of 40 or so to feed.

"Audra, I need you to start cutting up the fruit now. The first batch of chicken is about half done," I barked out.

"Ok, dad. Where are the knives?"

"And, Nancy, can you check on the potatoes? That oven is so old and unreliable, I'm not sure it's heating things evenly."

"Sure, I can do that," Nancy cheerfully responded.

"Oh my goodness, this grill is out of control. Can someone bring me a bucket of water? Quickly!"

Of course, part of the tradition was helping the process along with a few libations. The pace was intense, as was the heat from the grill. In the process, I had to admit that I lost track of the number of glasses of wine I had consumed. It was a delicious sauvignon blanc, by the way. By the time the family had been served, it was time for the kitchen crew to eat—but I had somehow wandered upstairs and found a bed to recline on, and was completely out. So much for getting to enjoy the nice dinner we'd prepared! Everyone was asking, "What happened to Tim? He was just here a few minutes ago." Nancy let them in on my secret: "Well, he started drinking wine at five!" Oh, my. The secret was out. Fortunately, I had no other destination than walking down the 100 stairs to the beach campfire that night.

As much as we might complain, express discontentment, or just plain make excuses for our "embarrassingly weird" families, I have been blessed to be a part of an extended family where we've done our best to overlook the failures and shortcomings of each other with a nod toward the greater goal of enjoying the "diversity" in our midst. Of course, we still have had our fair share of disagreements, misunderstandings, and moments of unpleasantness here and there. However, despite all the issues, we have managed to spend a lot of quality time together, learning from one another, and growing close together in a truly unique way—a definite rarity this day and age.

A significant part of this process was establishing a family tradition of an annual summer trip to Pentwater, Michigan. For twenty years—1991 to 2010—Mom and Dad Hoerr would book a week at the McVoy Cottage on the shores of Lake Michigan and invite each of my siblings, spouses, and kids to gather together. This was a one-of-a-kind property built as a summer home in 1917 by a wealthy industrialist from Chicago. It featured a large great room, a less-than-ideal kitchen by today's standards, a beautiful dining room, seven bedrooms, six bathrooms, and one shower in the basement! Perhaps the most memorable feature of the house was its spectacular views of Lake Michigan. Positioned on about ten acres of prime real estate, approximately 100 feet above the lake, it was a truly idyllic setting.

Reflecting on our family's commitment to getting together annually in Michigan, I've realized that there is great power, indeed life, in establishing and keeping traditions built around relationships. Of course, the practice of tradition is best kept in balance with everything else going on! For our family, we did indeed build a lifetime of memories around the annual summertime trip. While my parents, Jim and Virginia ("the Patriarchs" as they are affectionately known) would pay for the accommodations, my siblings and I were really the "owners" of the tradition.

We would take turns being the "Pentwater Czar," the designated organizer for a given year's trip. The czar's job was to do all of the planning in advance and prepare a newsletter with the valuable information for that year's trip. The Pentwater Hoerrald, as the newsletter was known, contained vital information like weather predictions, scheduled activities, menus for the planned meals, kitchen crew assignments, and of course, the highly anticipated room assignments. Not only that, but the Hoerrald grew over time to feature numerous articles written by nieces and nephews—usually recounting memorable incidents, inside jokes, and decidedly fabricated legends and lore from Pentwaters past.

I recall in particular that in 1994 there happened to be a number of mysterious occurrences in the old house, such as a rocking chair in the basement rocking and tipping over on its own, the appearance of a ghost face in one of the bedrooms, as well as a door that led to the attic appearing to swing open and shut by itself. These odd occurrences sparked the interest of some of the cousins to research the history of the house and what may have happened there.

Come to find out, the house was indeed listed under "The Haunted Heartland" list of houses and places in the area that were rumored to be haunted. As the story goes, a woman named Celeste was intended to be murdered in the house by her husband, but a spirit warned her of his evil intent and she was able to escape in time. Ah, whether it's true or not, it certainly added to the fun! The supposed haunted happenings of 1994, among many other more well-documented stories, were retold and rehashed playfully over the many summers at the house.

During our annual weeklong outings, we would experience life together as "one big group"—a group that now numbers over 70, including siblings, spouses, children, and grandchildren. As I shared above, a big part of the bonding time would come from cooking and sharing meals together, with each family member receiving an assignment (or multiple assignments) throughout the week. The kids often argued over who got too much work and who was able to avoid kitchen duty, and a few meals have gone down in history as being either "the best meal yet" or a "banned meal" (meatless spaghetti comes to mind).

We shared countless campfires on the beach together, complete with s'mores and stories, singing, and hanging out. The 20 years of Pentwater also held a few particularly special "traditions within the tradition." In addition to The Pentwater Hoerrald, we always enjoyed a vacation T-shirt, designed by one or more family members and distributed in advance of the trip—then worn for the annual family photo. I still have most of those T-shirts hanging in my closet somewhere. And, in a nod to our final year of doing Pentwater (yes, even the best traditions sometimes run their course), the design of the inaugural year (1991) T-shirt was revived and enhanced for the 20th and final year shirt, just for nostalgia's sake!

Another tradition we maintained was making a video of each year's adventures—in retrospect, a great way to relive the countless memories, quotes, jokes, and other escapades. Some members of the family (typically the third generation) have been known to watch and re-watch these videos to the point that they are the appointed experts of "all things Pentwater" (had to call you out on that one, AJ). One of the nephews, Philip, even created a Wiki site as a historical repository of all the goings-on! According to the Wiki site, there are over 200 inside jokes and sayings, and even more stories, from the 20 years of Pentwater vacations.

The question was often asked, was it the actual experience of the Pentwater vacation that was so great, or was it simply the memories that we still savor? Probably a bit of both, I imagine. The tradition of Pentwater created great anticipation in the family, the week itself offered great opportunities to "do life together," and the afterglow of memories has deeply impacted us all. I cannot imagine my children growing up without the meaningful interactions they've enjoyed with aunts, uncles, grandparents, and cousins in Pentwater. In fact, these rich experiences have shaped each of us, and they have become inherently part of who we are today. In the midst of the hustle and bustle of our busy lives, taking a week to reflect, relax, and connect with each other was valuable and renewing.

30. Kaley's Dilemma

Rural Arkansas, approximately 50 miles west of Little Rock
January 2011

THERE WERE EIGHT INCHES OF FRESHLY FALLEN SNOW COVERING THE HIGHWAY for miles on end, followed by a treacherous 100 miles of frozen slush, then another 100 miles of glazed ice. By the time I had counted 50 ditched or otherwise crashed vehicles—some quite horrifically—I stopped counting. A reasonable person would have thought we were in the middle of the frozen wilderness of Alaska, when in fact we were in Arkansas passing into Texas. And a reasonable person probably would have pulled off the road and decided to call it a day! But it was late on Sunday and classes were starting at 9 a.m. on Monday and my traveling companion, our youngest daughter Kaley, anxiously encouraged me to continue… so we carried on. In between reaching my left arm out of the driver's window to snap the windshield wiper to remove icy snow and Kaley calling out the GPS instructions for off-road mode, visions of newspaper headlines danced in my mind: "Idiot Father and College Daughter Found Buried in Snowbank," or "Wacky Dad and Teenage Daughter Slip-Slide Away on Remote Arkansas Road."

We had been driving for over 22 hours by the time we pulled into Waco, and the journey had been every bit out of a road trip disaster movie. What is normally a fairly comfortable 12- to 13-hour trip had turned into a white-knuckled, terror-filled, prayer-fueled odyssey. Just outside Little Rock, as the first inch or two of a snowstorm had kissed the interstate and begun to accumulate, we were stopped behind a long line of vehicles. Though we didn't know it at the time, a handful of big rigs had turned over a couple of miles ahead, completely blocking all west-bound traffic. After waiting for over two hours with little semblance of movement, a steady stream of cars was now turning around on the freeway, driving on the shoulders, heading back toward the nearest exit, about one mile to the east of where we had stopped. It was the first time I can remember dozens of cars pointing in the wrong direction on an interstate highway. Hesitant to join them, we called AAA and the state police to get some idea of our chances of forward progress. No luck.

Another hour went by and we reluctantly joined the wrong-way brigade, creeping toward the Social Hill, Arkansas exit ramp. Now what? We plotted a strategy to take a mishmash of roads that would get us back to I-30. A few miles in and we knew that no one else had chosen this particular strategy! Clearly, not a good sign. In fact, for the next two hours, we would traverse a variety of unplowed, two-lane roads with nearly 10 inches of snow and see almost no other traffic. That is, until we encountered the 40-degree grade portion of State Highway 84 in the middle of nowhere at about 8 p.m.

Here we were joined by a variety of other travelers—about eight to 10 cars stuck on the hill or in the adjacent ditches—and another five or six waiting at the bottom of the hill, deciding whether there was any chance of making it. We backed up about 75 yards and pulled off into a Pentecostal Church parking lot where a few locals had gathered.

"How ya doin' there, buddy?" A rather rotund man asked with a big smile.

"Not terribly well," I managed.

"Yer from Illinois?" He noted, looking at the car plate.

"Yes, sir."

"Where ya headed?"

"Trying to make it to Waco, Texas. My daughter's classes at Baylor start tomorrow."

"Ain't gonna make it tonight," he harrumphed.

"What do you mean?"

"What I mean is we don't get snow like this 'cept every seven years or so. This one's a doozy. See that hill up there?"

"I see it alright—that's why we turned back and pulled in here."

"Welp, I called for a tow truck about an hour ago. Trying to get them cars cleared off the hill. It's dangerous. Somebody gonna git kilt."

My spirits were flagging at this point. "Is there another way to get back to Interstate 30 West?"

"Nope. That's the only way. Gotta go up that hill. 'Course ya can't do that tonight. I'm gonna call the pastor to open up the church here. Ya might want to stay the night."

"Thanks for the offer. We'll think about it."

Kaley and I looked at each other, disheartened. We turned the car toward the hill, stopped, and looked at each other again. For some reason, in that moment, I sensed it was important to keep going. It would be a symbolic gesture to affirm a decision Kaley made only the day before—to return to Baylor when her heart was telling her otherwise (more on that later). It was in that moment that I realized the snowstorm and all of its obstacles were very real metaphors for the battle occurring in Kaley's mind and spirit. I knew that I had to press on.

"K, I know this sounds crazy, but I think we can make it," I said.

"I think we can too, Dad."

"Lord, we need you to clear out a path for us. Go ahead of us and make a way," I prayed out loud. Kaley nodded.

We waited for a few minutes. The eight to 10 cars on the hill were randomly scattered over 70 yards or so, covering nearly every portion of the road. I prayed again, silently this time. I looked up and saw movement on the hill. Not quite the parting of the Red Sea, but enough that a pathway appeared. I gunned the accelerator and literally zigged and zagged up the hill, narrowly steering clear of the assortment of stranded vehicles, avoiding two of them by inches—success!

"Ha! We did it, K!" I laughed out loud, with a few tears of joy thrown in for good measure.

"Dad, I can't believe you just did that!"

"Thanks, Lord. Stay with us on this!"

And indeed he did. Though a minor victory amidst the bigger battle, we both felt emboldened. We would need that extra dose of courage as we continued for another 45 minutes on this harrowing stretch, passing only one other car heading the other way on the two-lane asphalt. The snow, probably 10 to 12 inches deep, was starting to blow and drift. A previous car or two had left a set of tracks—but just barely. The shoulder of the road was indistinguishable from the highway, creating a sea of continuous whiteness. We didn't encounter a single snowplow (I suspect they don't have many in the state of Arkansas, and most likely not enough to handle a storm of that magnitude)—and one certainly hadn't been on this road since the storm began hours earlier. Other than moonlight reflecting off the snow and an occasional yard light shining in the distance, the cold blackness engulfed us. The sense of danger was tangible. The funny newspaper headlines I had earlier imagined took on a darker, more ominous tone as I replayed them in my mind. This was serious business.

Finally, with a groan of relief from us both, the on-ramp to I-30 West appeared. We learned later that the freeway had been officially closed, but there were no barriers erected at the on-ramp, so we (literally) plowed on. Our adventure was far from over, however as the miles of deep, unplowed snow gave way to 100 miles of crusty, bumpy, frozen slush. Those 100 miles probably took about three hours of white-knuckled navigation and violent shaking of the car, ultimately giving way to 100 miles of icy glaze as we approached Dallas. More cars in ditches. More cars overturned, wrecked. More imagined newspaper headlines taunting me. Finally, icy pavement turned to wet road, with temps hovering in the mid 30s.

Any other time in my life we would not have been crazy enough to even attempt this trip in this kind of weather and at this short of notice. But as I prayed and pondered the meaning of life along those last 75 miles into Waco, Texas I knew that something profound had unfolded in the last 48 hours, something that would remain with both Kaley and me for the rest of our lives.

From August, 2010, the beginning of her sophomore year at Baylor University, up to that fateful journey in early 2011, Kaley had been wrestling deeply with the decision to transfer home to Champaign and attend the University of Illinois. She had applied to Illinois and had been accepted into her program for a mid-year transfer effective January, 2011, yet she couldn't quite seem to muster the excitement or the conviction that this was the right decision for her. From my perspective, it seemed that the typical forces of a 19-year-old were driving her to consider coming home. A long-term, long-distance boyfriend for starters, and a very unhappy experience as a freshman at Baylor as she struggled with loneliness and being on her own for the first time. In the fall of 2010 she did in fact make new connections on the Baylor campus, with a local church and also with a handful of new friends. The boyfriend however, remained a prominent issue. He clearly wanted her to return home. And to me, that seemed to be the ultimate driving force behind her application to Illinois and her leaning toward that decision in late 2010 (and I'm quite sure now that this was an oversimplification of a very difficult life decision for Kaley!).

My oldest daughter, Alyssa, had made a college transfer decision six years earlier, attending Illinois State University for two years and then transferring to the U of I as a junior. I never doubted the decision she made, as it seemed to make all sorts of things fall into place for her. The circumstances were quite different for Kaley, of course—yet I found it ironic that my youngest daughter desired to enroll at Illinois and it seemed to me to be a huge mistake. Baylor fit her so well, and the experience of being far away from home had stretched and challenged her in ways that she was only beginning to realize. It seemed too soon to press the "abort mission" button and enroll at Illinois.

I have to admit that I wanted to flat out tell her—several times in fact—that I was convinced that transferring to Illinois was not the right decision for her. I resisted those temptations, sensing that it was important to honor her own decision-making process, and that my intervention in it could potentially have lifelong negative consequences. Meanwhile I was trying to be supportive and loving. But I couldn't completely alleviate her fears and concerns, nor could I offer the words she desired to hear: "Yes, come home, this is right for you."

At the conclusion of her December finals and the beginning of Christmas break, Kaley had still not made a final decision. For the trip home to Champaign, she filled her car with a variety of items from her campus apartment, but left most things behind in Texas. She had implemented what I now call the "parallel path plan"—enrolling at both Illinois and Baylor for the spring 2011 semester! When it came time to write the tuition check, however, that plan would be derailed. It was obvious to all of us how torn she was. Just a day or two before Christmas, she made the announcement of her final decision: She was transferring to Illinois. Alrighty then. Not what I had hoped, not by a long stretch. But it was time to be supportive of her decision and honor her adulthood by assisting her with a plan to get everything in place for being at Illinois for spring.

In the midst of that preparation, though, Kaley was dropping hints that her final decision perhaps was not so final. Little clues here and there, nothing major, but enough that I sensed something needed to be said. So, at the risk of scripting out a scenario for her, on the Thursday before classes were to begin on Monday I did make her an offer. Should she change her mind and return to Baylor after all, I would accompany her on the drive back, and I would arrange for a return flight for myself on Monday morning. She seemed nonplussed and gave neither a positive or negative response. Sort of a nod of the head and a bit of grunt. I assumed the issue was settled in her heart, but on Friday, I put a flight on hold just in case.

On Saturday afternoon, without saying a word, she began packing suitcases and boxes. I wandered upstairs and found her in the middle of what could best be described as a mess—the bedroom in a physical sense and from all observances, Kaley emotionally.

"Kaley, what's going on?"

"I'm not really sure. I'm packing." She looked confused.

"You're packing….so, you're going back to Baylor then?"

"I think so. Wait, I'm not sure. There's an apartment here in Champaign that I was looking at yesterday. Should we go take a look at that?"

"Go take a look at an apartment here in Champaign? But you're packing your bags for Baylor." Now I was confused.

"Well, I'm not sure. But I think I'm going to go back to Baylor."

"OK, should I take the hold off my return flight and book the ticket?"

"Umm… No."

"If I'm driving with you back to Baylor, I need to be able to get back. So…."

"I haven't spoken to Brian [not his real name]. I need to do that first."

Ah, now it was clear why there was still confusion in the mix. This was far from a settled issue, then. In fact, at that particular moment she seemed to have made a decision to do both! On one hand, she had already announced she was enrolling at Illinois. On the other hand, she was packing her bags for the return trip to Baylor. And on the third hand, she had yet to speak to her boyfriend about any of this.

Most of the drama that unfolded that evening I wasn't directly able to witness; it was more like sitting in a stadium with an obstructed view! First she entered into several hours of intense discussion with the boyfriend. Then she called me, saying little with long stretches of silence, interspersed with halting instruction to proceed with booking the flight. Then her call 30 minutes later to see if I had indeed done that, telling me she had changed her mind. I told her it was too late—that I had already booked the return flight and we would be leaving in the morning to drive her down. Late that Saturday evening, I heard the sobbing in the bedroom next to ours as she proceeded to pack boxes. And I heard about the "discussion" with her mother that appeared to be mostly heaving shoulders, crying, and several versions of "I can't do this," with lots of hugs thrown in for good measure.

At 6 a.m. Sunday morning, we were headed to Texas. The drama of the previous night would have a strong sequel, but in ways that played out quite surprisingly. Reflecting now on that adventurous trip, I can best describe it as a 22-hour microcosm that personified the challenge of making a tough decision and overcoming multiple obstacles along the journey.

It also resonates with me as a reminder of the powerful role that personal relationships play in our life decisions and how we act them out. How do we challenge and support those closest to us, while honoring and respecting them as individuals? Most importantly, I believe it is illustrative of an even bigger question: How do we make optimal decisions in the major points of inflection in our lives? How do we align our personal sense of purpose and calling with the "bigger picture"? Is the wrestling process as valuable as the decision itself? Is the journey as important as the destination? Are the important people in our life really engaged and along for the ride?

As I am finishing writing this chapter, Kaley has graduated from Baylor, having flourished in the final two-and-a-half years following her decision to return there in January of 2011. The relationship with the boyfriend has long since ended, and important to note, she has remained "single" since. She applied for and won a position as student ambassador through the highly competitive Baylor Student Foundation. She experienced her best academic years as a junior and senior. And, she is now enrolled in graduate school at St. Louis University.

Would it have played out similarly had she transferred to Illinois? Maybe. Maybe not. Am I thankful that I restrained myself from writing the script and dictating to her what I thought was the right decision? Absolutely. Did God insert himself into the process, nudging her to make the decision that was best? I'm convinced that he did. And, did he sovereignly intervene to protect Kaley and me—and knit our souls together in a profound way—on that treacherous trip?

No doubt.

31. Tuesday Morning Coffee Break

Champaign, Illinois
March 2011

PANERA BREAD, MATTIS AND KIRBY, 6:50 A.M., TUESDAY. A dusting of snow on the parking lot greeted me that morning, a few cars in the parking lot. Celia greeted me at the pastry counter with her big, toothy grin.

"Pumpkin muffie and a regular coffee, right?"

She had the order down cold.

"Yes, Celia. How are you today?"

"Well, I'm moving around and able to take nourishment! Now you, Tim, look a little sleepy this morning!"

It takes a special breed of person to have so much enthusiasm this early in the day, I've decided. God bless you morning people.

The crowd that day was a mix of the usuals—maybe 15 or 20 people that I recognized—and a smattering of others enjoying early morning conversation and a cup of joe. My brother Ben and I settled into one of the comfortable booths, with our pastries and coffee, to spend the next hour and half covering whatever comes to our minds. The earth-toned surroundings are comfortable, the mix of aromas pleasant, the companionship—as the credit card commercial says—priceless.

"Did you catch the any of the NCAA tourney games last night?" Ben asked.

"Oh my goodness. Upsets galore. This basketball tournament is sports at its absolute best."

"Too bad Illinois had to bow out against Kansas. You gotta hand it to the Selection Committee, putting Illinois in the same bracket as two of its former coaches, Bill Self and Lon Kruger!"

"Definitely. Made for a nice story.... Hey, shifting gears here for a minute, do you realize that we have about five weeks left of doing coffee before you and Tina hit the road to Peoria?" I asked.

"Been trying not to think of that, Tim. I might get weepy."

"I know I don't say it enough, so I'm going to say it now—thanks for being someone I can share pretty much anything with. I'm going to miss you."

"Gonna miss you too, man. Terribly. Three decades have passed in a blur."

"Sure have. There's been a lot of water under the bridge in that time, brother. Lots of highs. Definitely some lows. It's been really good to do it with you."

Life is difficult, as M. Scott Peck said right from the get-go in his book, The Road Less Traveled. One of the elements of navigating our way through life's challenges and difficulties is to build intimate, nourishing relationships with a few close friends. Seems simple, really. But genuine connections are difficult to find, and once found, nurturing them takes time and effort. The effort is worth it, as these are the relationships that can bring encouragement and strength to us when times are tough, and these are the confidants who can share in our joy when things are going well, without envy or competitive undercurrent. These are the relationships that can make us better, more thoughtful people and enrich our lives beyond measure.

For nearly 30 years (other than the four years we lived in San Diego and until May 2011, when he relocated), my brother Ben and I got together for coffee every Tuesday morning. The Tuesday morning coffee break became deeply woven into the fabric of both of our lives. It was a time that we both looked forward to, and looked back upon, each week, a time that other things were scheduled around. With Ben's relocation to Peoria, Illinois, our Tuesday morning coffee breaks have become less frequent—but every bit as meaningful. We're now doing our best to meet periodically in Bloomington, Illinois—sort of a half-way point between Peoria and Champaign.

During these interactions, we check in with each other on a wide range of topics: How our spouses and marriages are doing, what we thought about last night's ballgame, the latest news on our adult children's lives, what we think about a particular book, the state of affairs at each of our respective workplaces and churches, what we think Jesus really meant when he told the rich, young official "go sell all you have and give it to the poor," and when we're going to check out the new brew pub.

We tend to probe the depths of life's bigger questions, while at the same time covering more lighthearted fare. This is what makes our interaction and relationship truly meaningful, and might I say, authentic. We cover the meat of the matter but also take time to celebrate life's little pleasures and stuff that isn't too serious. I like to think of our time together as replenishing and nourishing. If I come into one of our get-togethers feeling the weight of the world, I often leave feeling refreshed and energized. And If I arrive at one of our morning interactions with a bounce in my step, I hope that I can have an encouraging impact on Ben by sharing some of my good news. Come to think of it, regardless of what each of us is encountering in any given week, we tend to raise the spirits of the other.

Reflecting on the major decisions I've faced over the last three decades—and many of the minor ones—nearly every one of them got processed, examined, discussed, and bantered about with Ben, and most of them in the context of the Tuesday Morning Coffee Break. Which job to take out of college in 1983. Later that same year, whether the romantic relationship with Toni had the makings of a solid marriage (the answer was a resounding "yes," by the way!). In 1989, whether to remain in the accounting profession or seek some other path. Whether to relocate to San Diego in 1995, or remain in the comfort and familiarity of Champaign. And then whether to move back to Illinois in 1999.

Whether to stay in the business world when my professional life was falling apart later that same year. Buying a one-third interest in Gameday Spirit in 1999 when we'd done nothing but drain our savings accounts in the 18 months prior. Co-founding iCyt in 2001. And leaving there in 2008. Countless other critical inflection points—all exposed to the light of Ben's perspective and counsel. In many ways, these decisions deeply impacted and changed me. They are part and parcel of the person I've become. So you might say that I am who I am in large part due to the counsel and guidance of my brother, sharing life over a cup of coffee one interaction at a time.

A relationship like this can often act as an oasis amidst the sea of draining and difficult relationships we otherwise find ourselves in. All around us are work colleagues, customers, family members, or the neighbors next door—many of whom require our energy, time, and attention, but don't seem to reciprocate in a positive way. In fact, many of these relationships are one-sided and therefore life-sapping. Because of this imbalance, it is important to have relationships that do just the opposite, relationships that build us up and provide us encouragement. I call these "nourishing relationships" because they feed our soul, lift our vision, and catalyze our personal growth. And while these relationships may be hard to find and develop, the payback is rich indeed.

32. Mark Shannon: A Brilliant Flame Gone Too Soon

Urbana, Illinois
October 2012

O**N A CRISP FALL DAY, WE GATHERED TO SAY OUR FINAL GOODBYES** to Mark Shannon. Several hundred friends, colleagues, and family members packed the smallish church on Green Street in Urbana. We shared warm embraces and exchanged pained expressions. We cried and laughed throughout the powerful eulogy. The intimate stories shared by Mark's son, his brother-in-law, and others were poignant—and reminded many of us of our own Mark Shannon stories. He was a person who had become intimately connected with many of us, changing our lives for the better. He was, indeed, an extraordinary man who slipped from our midst far too early.

I first met Mark when he interviewed me as I was being considered for the role of transitional CEO for his start-up company, Cbana Labs. Cbana creates novel, micro-scale gas analyzers for detection of toxic, explosive, and polluting materials. I guess you would call it an interview, but in over an hour, I might have answered one or two questions. For the balance of the time, Mark was enthusiastically sharing with me his passion for this technology, the scientists working on it, and its potential for making the world a better place. He was doing his best to cover all the bases in the short time that we had together, which left little time to do what I thought we were supposed to be doing! That initial encounter provided pretty keen insight into the person of Mark Shannon.

Passionate.

Committed.

Enthused.

A technologist. A professor. A humanitarian.

At the time of the interview, Mark was impressively juggling a number of high-level commitments, including director of the University of Illinois Center of Advanced Materials for the Purification of Water with Systems, mechanical engineering professor, cofounder and chief scientific officer of Cbana Labs, as well as the roles of devoted husband and father to three young men. You could say he was spinning a few plates—and he was pretty good at it!

I liked the fact that despite all of his impressive credentials, Mark wasn't a bragger, didn't come off as superior to those around him, and in fact, went out of his way to encourage and coax the best out of everyone he came in contact with. And, I liked that Mark was constantly exploring new ways to do things, and always learning how to apply some newfangled research technique to a practical problem we were solving at Cbana. Mark was also a guy that remembered his humble beginnings as a machinist and tradesman. He was always eager to point out his official "PhD," a workman's post-hole-digger, which he kept in his office for all to see. True to his roots, he was always one to roll up his sleeves to help our team tackle difficult technical problems.

All of this being said, it was incredibly difficult to accept that Mark was diagnosed with and eventually succumbed to Amyotrophic Lateral Sclerosis (ALS), otherwise known as Lou Gehrig's disease, named for the famous baseball player from the 1920s and '30s. For those who are not familiar, ALS is a horrible disease of the nerve cells in the brain and spinal cord that control voluntary muscle movement. In ALS, nerve cells waste away or die and can no longer send messages to muscles. This eventually leads to muscle weakening, twitching, and an inability to move the arms, legs, and body. Slowly, all muscle function is lost. Speaking becomes difficult and eventually impossible. Meanwhile, the mind remains vibrant and functional until the very end—but is imprisoned in a physical body that refuses to function normally. There is no cure for ALS, and most victims pass away within three to five years of diagnosis.

Mark started experiencing symptoms of ALS in early 2009 and a diagnosis of the disease was officially confirmed in summer of 2010. He began losing significant motor control as the fall and winter seasons progressed. What once were simple tasks, such as shampooing his hair and carrying his laptop computer, became impossible. During this difficult time and until October 14, 2012, Mark valiantly fought the disease with an attitude nothing short of remarkable.

Though he accepted what the disease was doing to him physically, he refused to "check out" and focus on himself. On the contrary, he remained as engaged as possible in the work of Cbana and continued to be involved in the lives and work of his PhD students at the university. He had just commenced teaching his latest course for grad students in the fall of 2012, just weeks before his death. His University of Illinois department chair, Placid Ferreira, shared, "I cannot begin to express in words how indebted our department is to Mark. A true visionary, Mark was an extraordinary person who dedicated his work and efforts to our students. He was an inspiration to all of us and we will always remember his generosity and strength. He will be missed in every facet of our academic endeavor."

In a visit to his home in August, 2012, his eyes were lit up with excitement as he communicated with me through his computer and a lip-reading nurse about the importance of continuing his work and his involvement in the lives of others. In fact, he told me that he firmly believed that God was extending his life, even in physically and emotionally debilitating form, for some very specific reasons. He wanted my opinion on a new patent disclosure he was working on. He was curious, too, about Cbana's technical progress on the NASA project. And, he wanted to know how my family was doing. In a parting moment, he expressed optimism about continuing to interact with and impact those around him.

Wow. Talk about a selfless and inspiring example.

During the last three years of his disease progression, Mona, his wife of thirty-plus years, embraced her role of caregiver, confidant, and navigator of strange, uncharted waters with incredible grace. Her resolve to make the best of a challenging situation was so encouraging. Her blog posts shared candidly about life-threatening encounters with ventilators that stopped working, equipment alarms ringing at 2 a.m., and health care aides that were befuddled with situations they had never seen before. Both before and during this challenging struggle, those who knew Mona and Mark could easily see the deep commitment they had for one another. And though tested as never before, they really did confront the battle with aplomb—and in the process, they helped the rest of us to cope.

Mark's life was a true inspiration to me. Here was someone who not only knew his calling, but was living it out with gusto. Never satisfied with the status quo, Mark was always pushing himself and everyone around him to grow, to do better, and to stretch. He was ever in search of colleagues and partners who would share his thirst for excellence, for learning, and for continuous improvement. To be in relationship with Mark was to be challenged, to be awakened, and to be catalyzed.

And so, I am left wondering how Mark could have been taken from us at the young age of 56. And how could someone like Mark be consigned to suffer with such a horrible disease? Is there meaning in Mark's horrific suffering and death? What fairness is there in such a bright, compassionate fireball—one of the most passionate human beings I've known—having his world upended and ultimately his life snuffed out in its prime?

These are troubling questions. Nevertheless, the questions must be asked—and indeed, they do demand answers. So, I've asked the questions over and over in my mind, and I've posed them out loud to friends. I've asked the questions in my prayers to the Lord, alone, on my backyard deck.

Slowly, over the last several months of asking and waiting, the answers have been forthcoming. Not terribly clear ones. And not neat, tidy, black-and-white answers, either. More like paradoxical riddles that coax me to push deeper, to probe farther, and to go beyond simple life principles and platitudes. The riddles put me in an uneasy place, a place of discomfort. Riddles such as "life will always have a component of mystery to it, so embrace the mystery," and "face your fears, accept that there is much about life that's unknowable, allow Me to be God, even if you don't understand Me," and "treasure the time you had with Mark and accept his challenge to never stop growing." Those are far from satisfactory answers, I know. But they are a start.

In the asking of these questions and the mulling over of the slowly emerging answers, Mark's life and death have taken on a deeper, more profound meaning. The process has caused me to stop and reevaluate why I am doing what I'm doing, and I believe that's a healthy thing. Knowing him and remembering him have caused me to evaluate the bigger purpose to which I'm called, and to which each of us is called—and ask myself whether I'm laying it all out there to "go for it" as Mark did.

The last few years with Mark brought me a new appreciation for the power and importance of relationships, for spending time with those connected to us. The interactions with Mark in his living room—me on the couch feeling powerless to help, he in the wheelchair, connected to a ventilator, showing me strength and fire with a glint in his eyes—taught me that an intimate, tender connection to another human being is one of the most powerful things on earth. Remembering him today brings me to a place of weeping and wondering, grateful for the opportunity to wrestle at a deeper level with life's most difficult questions, blessed by the beauty of the world in which we live… and ultimately die.

Thank you, Mark. Godspeed.

33. Worship, Pray, Give

Austin, Texas
May 1984

TEXAS MEMORIAL STADIUM, the largest and most state-of-the-art facility in the Southwest, was bustling with track athletes at the 1984 Southwest Conference Championships. As darkness fell, the stadium lights burned bright, illuminating sprinters, long jumpers, hurdlers, throwers, and distance runners there to compete at one of the highest levels in college sports. Some of the most talented athletes were gathered from across the country in what would be a memorable night.

David Hodge, a sophomore from Baylor University, was one of the favorites in the pole vault. Now, a certain wackiness is required for anyone competing in this true fan-favorite field event—and David possessed a unique combination of zaniness, talent, fearlessness, and competitive drive. Pole vaulters run at top speed for about 30 yards, plant a 16-foot fiberglass pole in the plant box, invert their bodies skyward while bending the pole, and twist in such a manner as to "clear the bar," with the goal of cleanly clearing and landing safely in the vault pit on the opposite side. At each bar height, competitors have three tries to clear. The bar is then raised to the next height. The pole vault attracts so many fans because of the extreme physical and mental challenges it presents, combined with the element of danger and increasing drama as the bar is raised to each new height.

1984 was an Olympic year, and David had high hopes of making the Olympic team. Earlier that season, he had cleared 17'9", sufficient to qualify him to participate in the Olympic Trials later that summer. That particular mark was David's career best. With the mental component of vaulting as important as, and perhaps more so, than the physical, could Hodge go on to win the Southwest Conference Championship? By 8:15 p.m. that evening, David had encountered some roadblocks and was in second place. The bar was raised to 18'0". He would need a new personal record to win.

On his first attempt, David clipped the bar with his foot and it tumbled off the standard. The second attempt was close, but again unsuccessful, the bar clanging to the ground. It was now do or die—one final attempt.

David stood at the end of the runway, gathered his thoughts and uttered a brief prayer. Gripping the pole, he gazed resolutely forward, mentally locked in. "Through Christ, I can do anything." He ran with a sense of power and determination. Without breaking stride, he planted the pole. His body soared upward. Body twisting, turning. Clearing the bar with room to spare. Kerploosh. He landed in the pit, immediately springing to his feet, lifting both arms in jubilation. With that jump, David had won the conference championship. But he did not stop there. The bar was then raised to 18'2½"—a height that would be a conference record and the all-time highest jump in SWC history. With the championship already in the bag, David felt loose and confident. It was time to reach for the stars.

It only took one attempt at 18'2½"—and David's name was in the record books.

The celebration began in earnest. David was immersed into a crazy, joyful milieu of coaches, teammates and family members, with back slaps, hugs, and high fives all around. What an amazing night! What incredible fun! But amidst the cacophony, David paused in a moment of quiet reflection. He paused to do something that had become routine for him—to worship, acknowledging the ultimate source of his strength. In some sense, David's incredible performance that night was in itself an act of worship. He had trained incredibly hard, fully using his God-given talents to accomplish something no one else in the Southwest Conference had ever done.

When any of us give our all in that way, it is indeed worship. It's what the scriptures say is the primary mission of humankind. In worship, we acknowledge the one who is really in control, the source of all life, love, and purpose. In recognition that David's talent was a gift from the Creator and his accomplishment that night was infused by the power of God's spirit, David turned his face heavenward, worshipping with a heart of gratefulness.

I met David the first or second week after his move to Champaign, Illinois, in late 1990. Terry Snyder, a partner in McGladrey and Pullen, and I invited David to lunch after learning that he had been hired as the new controller of one of our key clients, Gill Athletics. A world-famous manufacturer of track and field equipment, Gill had struggled in the '70s and '80s and was teetering toward financial collapse. David explained over burgers at the Bombay Bicycle Club in Urbana that the president of Gill had tracked him down in Eugene, Oregon, and asked him to consider moving to Illinois to help the struggling company. By that time, David's athletic career had been derailed by injury (just prior to the 1988 Olympics!), he had completed his MBA, and he was looking for interesting opportunities in business. For someone who had already enjoyed a "career" as a student and professional athlete, the chance to align himself with a new career in the sporting equipment industry was intriguing. The financial condition of the company notwithstanding, David and his wife Amy decided it was a good fit for them. So with infant daughter Heather in tow, they moved cross country to the exciting flatlands of corn and soybeans.

There was pretty much an instant connection between David and me during our brief luncheon that day. It was obvious to me that he brought a great deal of competence to the challenging job at Gill. Equally compelling—and also obvious—was his strong faith and quiet confidence. I extended an invitation for David and Amy to visit our couple's small group that following Friday evening. Eager to meet others in their new surroundings, David enthusiastically said yes.

I don't recall the topic of discussion that Friday night, but when we broke into groups of four or five to talk and pray together, David and I ended up in the same mini-group. In those 30 minutes, our connection grew deeper. Both of us were asking the same questions: "How do I become more like Jesus?" and "How does my story connect to his?" We both shared a desire to integrate faith and business. We both aspired to be leaders of others. We each wanted to bring honor to God by being focused and diligent in all aspects of our lives. We exchanged a warm smile and an embrace as the evening concluded; we knew at that moment that our lives were destined to intersect with and sharpen one another.

David and I began meeting regularly, sharing with each other about our work, our visions for the future, our families, and the inner recesses of our personal lives. No topic was off limits. Pretty powerful medicine in a world where masks are routinely worn to hide the real issues and difficulties in our lives. I'm not saying we did it without a hitch here and there, but it's something we're still doing, nearly a quarter-century later. We've worked through problems together, discussed relationship challenges, and celebrated our successes. A nice bonus, our spouses became very good friends along the way.

David's worshipful lifestyle challenged me from the get-go to surrender myself more completely to God. He exhibited a way of doing life that I would describe as "all in." He held nothing back. Worship, of course, is necessarily intertwined with prayer. And early in our friendship, I discovered David's intentional commitment to this powerful spiritual discipline.

Soon after his arrival in Champaign, the company's bank notes were called, putting it on the brink of bankruptcy. A local investor, Vince Atkins, stepped in to assume responsibility for the debt and take over ownership of the failing enterprise. Vince requested that David meet with him. Driving to Vince's office, a number of thoughts danced in David's head as he worked through a variety of worst-case scenarios. David took a deep breath, praying silently but with determination as he entered Vince's office.

"Take a seat, David." Vince gestured toward the couch. "Thanks for coming to see me, I appreciate it."

"Sure, Vince." After all, you are the owner, David thought to himself.

"The company's in bad shape, David. You know that." Vince spoke calmly, firmly. He looked directly into David's eyes. David expected Vince's next sentence to be his dismissal.

"I'd like you to consider taking the helm of Gill Athletics, David. I've been impressed with your leadership, and I believe you're the man for the job."

David was completely taken off guard. Having expected his firing, he was being asked to take on the role of CEO.

"Vince, I don't know what to say… I…" David, bewildered, couldn't even finish his sentence.

"David, I know it's a lot to think through. But if you'll become the CEO and turn this company around, I'll promise you the opportunity to buy the company from me some day," Vince said.

Being intimately familiar with the company's disastrous shape, David felt a sense of nausea overtake him. Instinctively, David knew this was a situation beyond his natural capabilities, gifted though he was.

After agreeing to accept the CEO position, David began a ritual that continues to this day, putting a list of prayers on his office white board. It was a list of very practical issues that needed to be solved if the company were to survive and ultimately grow. A voluntary management team prayer meeting was also begun, as David looked for divine guidance to turn the company around. The next four years were incredibly difficult, with numerous problems confronting David and his team on a daily basis. Wholesale changes were made in the way the business was run, but the results were still disappointingly poor. David kept thinking "we're doing things right; we're not this bad!" But the bottom line was saying otherwise. He continued to persevere in prayer.

By 1994, David was at the end of his wits. He sought counsel from his dad as they walked together in the woods outside the family home in Mt. Vernon, Illinois. He broke down sobbing in his dad's arms, and resolved to quit the position of CEO of Gill Athletics. It was time for someone else to take a swing at making it work.

At this lowest of low points, "God showed up and answered my prayers," as David describes it. Tom Burtness, a friend from the Vineyard Church, encouraged David to "move your margins"—in other words, increase pricing. This counter-intuitive strategy seemed to be the last thing that would really work, but David and his team had tried everything else. With the new catalog set to be priced and printed within weeks, the timing of Tom's encouragement seemed spot-on. David followed through on the advice, and breakthrough occurred. The company's bottom line turned from red to black that year—and started a string of profitability that extends to this day. Gill Athletics has returned to the number one position in the world in the track and field industry. Along the way, David was able to purchase the company from Vince. He went on to acquire Porter Athletic (maker of basketball and volleyball equipment, among other items), and merged both companies into a new holding company, Litania Sports Group. Litania is Latin for "list of prayers."

It's obvious to many of us who know David that he exemplifies an entrepreneur with an unusual commitment to worship and prayer. He is unashamed to stand in front of an audience to declare the ultimate source of his strength and to describe how he taps into that source. His life has been built on the premise of surrendering control to God on a daily basis through these two disciplines, acknowledging that there is a bigger story into which his story fits. That really is the essence of worship and prayer—turning our focus outward, toward the Creator of the universe, inviting him to accomplish his larger purposes through us.

But there is yet a third "weapon" in David's spiritual business arsenal. It's one that he's not very comfortable talking about, for good reason. But having known him for nearly 25 years, I've been able to observe his generosity first hand. David is a giver. Even in very lean times, David has always committed a meaningful portion of his resources to people, causes, and organizations that rely on charitable support. In fact, he credits the prosperity of his life and business to a long-standing practice of regular, sacrificial giving. In a recent conversation with David, I explored the mystery of how David has prospered by "giving away" as opposed to "holding on."

"It's one of the most counter-intuitive scriptural principles, Tim," David said.

"What do you mean by that?"

"Conventional wisdom would say, be very judicious and keep close tabs on your precious, limited resources. If there's extra, put it away for a rainy day. But God's wisdom says be generous. Freely give."

"That does seem to fly in the face of worldly wisdom," I said.

"And the strange thing is, the more we give away, the more God seems to give back to us. Not always in the same way. In the end, we end up the benefactor—with more abundance than we could imagine."

In the last 30-plus years, David has experienced incredible fruitfulness in all phases of his life. It's not been without a considerable amount of hardship along the way. There have always been obstacles to overcome, some of them quite daunting. His life example has been a real encouragement to me and to countless others. I believe he has had, and continues to have, a special influence because of the authenticity of his story. And at the center of David's entrepreneurial story is a trio of "secret weapons"—a commitment to worship, pray, and give.

PART 4

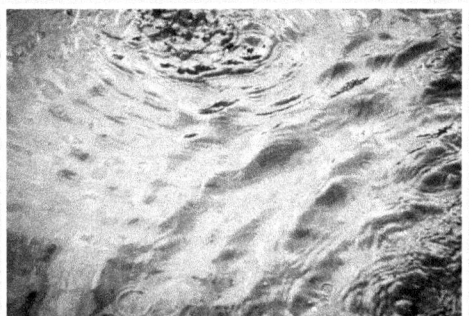

Reflections

One phrase I often use in conversations with colleagues and clients is "getting the view from 30,000 feet." It's about seeing the larger perspective, intuiting the bigger themes, grasping the more comprehensive picture in any given situation. This final part of the book is a collection of thoughts and musings from the view at 30,000 feet.

34. Inflection Points

Peoria, Illinois
July 1978

THOUGH IT HAPPENED ON A SULTRY AFTERNOON IN JULY so many years ago, I can still smell the strange mixture of asphalt, oil, Illinois cornfields, and broken rolls of sod. I can hear the explosion of crunching metal and shattering glass amidst chaos, the eerie silence immediately after, followed within minutes by the wail of sirens. I can feel the 90-degree summer heat, the moisture in the air, and the sweat on my face. I can vividly see the surreal scene of the flatbed sod truck I was driving moments earlier, flipped completely over 30 yards or so from the intersection; the Pontiac four-door with the front end completely demolished; the driver of the Pontiac covered in blood, barely conscious, moaning. I can remember walking away from the Pontiac, away from the bloodied driver, a middle-aged woman. I can recall a consuming sense of shock and bewilderment. A sense that life would not be the same on the other side of this tragedy.

Earlier that day, I was tasked with delivery 120 yards—two full pallets—of freshly cut sod to the Caterpillar facility in Pekin, Illinois. I was young (16), barely licensed to drive. I was also bold, self-assured—and unwilling to ask for proper directions (apparently, this character trait is shared by many—most?—of the male gender). In an era well before GPS and Google Maps, I failed to consult a map or someone who knew the route before departing Hoerr's Nursery for what would be an ill-fated journey. I had a vague notion of where Pekin was—but only that. Having lost my way about 30 minutes in, I stopped to ask for directions at a gas station.

"Can I help you, kid?" The attendant with his smudged baseball cap smiled at me wryly.

"Uh... I think... well, I'm lost."

"Where ya goin?"

"Trying to find the Cat plant in Pekin, Illinois. Am I anywhere close?"

"Well, kinda. I reckon you're not too far off."

"That's what I figured. Can you help me with directions?"

"Don't have a map handy, I'm afraid. What you need to do is turn right up here on Smithville Road—then take another right on Cameron Road. Take that until it dead-ends on 24. You'll see the sign for Pekin there. Take a left on 24 and a right on 9."

"Thanks, mister."

Redirected and then on an unfamiliar stretch of rural road, I was driving the truck at 60 miles per hour, trying to make up time. In a simultaneous nano-moment of recognition, I saw a car cross the highway 25 yards in front of me while seeing that I had a stop sign. There was no time to react, to hit the brakes. In the next instant, the truck's cab was a nightmare mixture of flying shards of glass, a cacophony of horrible sounds, and exploding, twisting metal. It lasted all of five seconds, and then... complete and eerie silence. I was upside down in what remained of the crushed truck cab. The steering wheel was pulled loose from its stem. In a state of semi-shock, I noted that all of my limbs were intact and that I was still breathing. With only minor bruises and scrapes, I crawled from the cab's open window into the grassy drainage ditch.

Fifty years of life experience has taught me that there are important times in our lives where we are offered an opportunity to join ourselves to something bigger, to hear God speaking to us, to awaken to the larger reality in which our lives operate. It was in the aftermath of the crash that I experienced such a moment. Day-to-day life was suspended for those few days immediately following the accident. There was a gravity, a depth of emotion that I had never before experienced. I was consumed with the life-altering impact I'd had on another person and her family (thankfully, after a short hospital stay, she was fine). As I pondered what it meant to be alive, to have survived a horrific crash against the odds, I heard an invitation. I sensed that there was purpose to be accomplished and a unique reason for my being. It seemed to me that I had been spared because there was something I was destined to do, something that would have gone undone had I died. It was time to more intentionally connect my story to God's story.

While the deeper "life aha's" were revealing themselves to me, I did have some very practical stuff to deal with in the short run! Like a visit from State Trooper McGruder (not his real name), who had been at the accident scene. He stopped by our home on Evergreen Circle in Peoria about two days later.

"Timothy, you are one lucky young man," he said with a deep-throated voice.

"Yes, sir, I believe that."

"That was an ugly accident, son. In examining your truck afterwards, I don't see how you survived."

"Yes, it was horrible. I'm thankful to be alive. I don't know what else to say."

"Well, probably not much to say. I do have a ticket here for you, though. I've combined the multiple charges onto one ticket—running a stop sign, driving too fast for conditions."

"Yes, sir. I'm thinking of giving up driving altogether, officer."

"Now look, Timothy—or is it Tim? You're a good young man. This accident has impacted you in a strong way—I can tell that. Now, use this awful experience to learn from it. But don't use it as cop-out."

I smiled gratefully at him. "Okay, I think I get that."

"Good. I'm sure your parents would say the same thing, son."

"Sir, how is the lady doing?" I'd been thinking constantly about her, hoping she was okay.

"She's doing okay. She's recuperating at Proctor Hospital. I'd say you both are pretty lucky."

I breathed easier, hearing she was going to be okay. "Divine luck, if there is such a thing, sir."

Yes, there were some practical things to process and work through—the moving violation, the increased insurance rates, overcoming my fear about getting back behind the wheel, a lawsuit which inevitably followed, depositions with attorneys and insurance companies, and a financial settlement with Mrs. Broderick that helped us all avoid a jury trial about a year later. But amidst the weeds of these day-to-day challenges was a growing sense of invitation from the Creator to join him in a lifelong adventure. To join my unique mixture of passion, talent, and life experience to something meaningful and eternal—and to Someone.

I believe that each of us will receive one or more such invitations, though they will likely arrive in a manner as unique as each of our individual purposes. The invitations will often arrive in what I call an inflection point. These are singularly unique moments in our lives that are distinguished from the ordinary. My brother Ben describes them as the coat hooks upon which the balance of our life experience hangs. In these moments, if we will apprehend them and wrestle with them, we can begin to comprehend a new and meaningful way that our lives were meant to count for something more than just plotting our own course to personal happiness. That we are indeed unique, irreplaceable in the sense that a calling awaits us that is uniquely for us, unable to be fulfilled by any other person.

In addition to awakening our spirits in regard to a personal purpose, God also uses inflection points to encourage us and provide us specific direction for our lives. This guidance can come to us in a variety of ways, as I've shared throughout this book. Sometimes, God shows up with skin on.

Fast forward from 1979 to 2003. I remember a slight breeze blowing, temps in the mid 70s, and floral scents from a variety of tropical species delighting my senses. The lanai was the perfect place for a cup of morning joe, in what was our last full day on Kaanapali Beach in Maui, Hawaii. From my vantage point, the surf appeared pretty active that day, with early morning sun bouncing in a playful fashion off the waves.

It was April, 2003, and the spring break week had been a welcome respite from the Illinois winter. Over the course of the week, Toni, Alyssa, Audra, Kaley, and I had snorkeled amidst a dazzling panorama of fish, coral, and seaweed; we'd driven the snaking highway to Hana through some of the most lush tropical forest our kids had ever seen; we'd enjoyed fresh seafood and lots of pineapple, mango, and other flavor-rich fruits; and we'd been to the obligatory luau with fire-handlers, hula dancers, unlimited (watered-down) mai tais, tasty roast pig, and a smorgasbord of delicious local fare. But perhaps our favorite activity that week was the non-activity of lounging at the beach and pool, soaking up the sun and enjoying each other's company.

Since it was the last day we would spend in Maui, Audra (then 15), Kaley (12), and I headed out for some fun in the waves. Though we asked Toni and Alyssa (18) to join us, they preferred to stay poolside. After staking out our ground on the beach, we sprinted into the ocean. The water was warm and inviting, the waves active and exciting. There was little clue of the impending danger in which we would soon find ourselves.

After 30 minutes of frolic, we were all feeling a bit tired, and I called out to the girls that we should start to head back in. It was then that I realized for the first time that we were quite a distance from the shore—perhaps 100 yards or so. Funny, I didn't think we'd actually swum that far out. And we hadn't, really.

About five minutes into our swim toward shore, it was dawning on me that we were not getting any closer to the sand. In fact, we seemed to be farther out—maybe 130 or 150 yards by then. We were swimming with determination, each of us having had quite a bit of swimming experience, and the girls involved in regular athletic activities to keep them in top shape (me, that was another story!). We were beginning to breathe hard, fighting harder against the swells, taking in gulps of saltwater. Another five minutes, and we realized that we were going nowhere. Our bodies were aching, muscle strength was flagging, and now we were struggling to stay above the strong surf. I gathered the girls close to me to try and hold them up, while also trying to swim forward. I began to see the panic in their eyes. I realized at that moment that we were in incredible danger.

As the reality of the moment gripped me, the awful thought entered my mind that we may not make it back to shore. We may, I thought to myself, be close to drowning. By this time my head was barely bobbing above the surface, trying to buoy the girls.

Desperate, I let out an audible prayer—"Jesus!"

"Dad, what's going to happen to us?" Kaley cried.

"Are we going to drown?" Audra asked, fear threading her voice.

"Jesus!" I yell again, with singular focus, louder.

"Jesus!" Louder still.

It was then that I noticed a tall, dark-haired man with brown swim trunks about 20 yards from us—funny thing, that I could see his swimming trunks, with all of his torso above the waves, though we must have been in water that was at least 15 to 25 feet deep.

"HELP! We need help!" I yelled to the man in the brown swim trunks.

He smiled back at me, saying nothing. Doesn't he get it, I thought? Can't he see we are close to dying?

"We need HELP! We are drowning!" I yelled louder.

Again, he smiled as if everything was completely normal and under control—and calmly called back, "Sometimes it helps if you swim at a different angle."

What? This crazy guy obviously sees that a man and two children are drowning, and all he can offer up is some swimming advice? Thanks, buddy, but with help like that that, we'll all be goners in the next three to five minutes.

But instantly it hit me—a deep memory resurrected from my lifesaving training as a teenager—when you are caught in a rip tide, swim parallel to the shore! Or, in essence, swim at a different angle! In the panic of exhausted swimming, terrorized by the thought of losing my daughters, I had not realized that we were caught in a strong rip current, flowing at a very high speed and with incredible force sweeping us away from shore. I realized it later, of course, but my brain had not been functioning properly in the moment of crisis. And I suppose that's normal in times of extreme distress—we dispense with logic, our brains freeze up, and we operate on emotion and adrenaline.

"Girls, we need to start swimming sideways. NOW!"

"What do you mean, Dad?"

"Swim parallel to the shore, not toward it—follow me," I said, gripping each of them again and tugging them along.

In less than two minutes, we were free from the clutches of the rip current. I looked toward "Mister Swimming Advice" and watched him do a complete body flip, disappearing into the waves. Audra, Kaley, and I headed toward shore, swimming easily. We collapsed on the sand, none of us was able to speak for perhaps five minutes. We were shaking, exhausted. We each realized the gravity of what had just gone down—that we were minutes from death when someone with brown swimming trunks and dark hair offered us swimming advice—and, indeed, saved us.

There was power and the poignancy in that moment. We hugged each other. Kaley was still unable to speak, even after gathering her strength and her wits. I, too, was slow to verbalize my thoughts, still shaken by the "what if." Audra was the first to say it.

"Dad, who was that man?"

"I don't know, honey."

"How did he do that flip?"

"That's a really good question. We were in deep water, Audi, and he seemed to be standing on something when he flipped."

"Was he an angel?"

"Seems possible. Maybe. Probably."

"Where did he go?"

"I don't see him anywhere," I said.

And it is then that I realized that it most certainly was someone from an alternate reality—breaking into our world of three dimensions to save us. Not in the manner that we had expected, of course. But in a way that was just as useful. We slowly gathered up our towels and headed toward the swimming pool. Shaken. Tired. Thankful.

I've thought of this event often in the succeeding years—now more than 10 years ago. I've grown more convinced that we were indeed rescued that day by nothing short of God's incredible intervention. Left to our own capabilities (which were not functioning that well), our own strategy (swim forward!), and our own strength (essentially, depleted to the point of nothing left), we most surely would have succumbed to drowning in the course of another few minutes.

Though I grew up in a church with a fairly precise definition of what it meant to "be saved"—and nearly all of my life have been involved in Christian circles with explicit definitions for that phrase—the near-drowning experience brought a whole new understanding and dimension of meaning to those words. We had been saved afresh and given a new lease on life. We had been rescued by God with skin on—not physically intervening per se, but gently smiling and instructing us what to do.

Just like the 1979 truck crash, this surreal experience served as an inflection point for my family and me. Through it, I again considered the larger framework within which my life was unfolding and pondered how to best steward my time, energy, and talents. I specifically thought about what it would mean to "swim at a different angle" in the metaphorical sense. Was there anything I was currently doing that needed to be re-examined, adjusted, changed?

In subsequent years, the solemnity of the experience has created a rich sense of gratefulness in me. It has catalyzed and deepened my understanding of personal purpose and how it ultimately fits into a bigger story controlled by the Creator. And it has given me an awe-filled reverence for God's intimate love and concern for each of us. It is perhaps one of the most encouraging pieces of news I've ever encountered—that God is inviting each of us, with our unique and highly personal stories, to join the bigger story of stewarding the creation.

We may not always recognize him and his invitation. He may not communicate with us in the way we expect. He may offer instruction which at first seems hard to understand or perhaps even uncaring, considering our dire circumstances. But if we hear what he has to say, if we embrace the moment of intimacy, if we are willing to act in accordance with his instruction and align our story with his, our lives will become immeasurably enriched.

35. Like Good Wine, Most Things in Life Take (a Long) Time

Waco, Texas
May 2012

OUR MIDDLE DAUGHTER AUDRA CROSSED THE FER-RELL CENTER STAGE a few years ago, along with family friend Heather Hodge and a few thousand classmates, in the Baylor University Class of 2012. Ken Starr, the president of Baylor, encouraged the graduates with mountain-climbing analogies and some good ole common sense. More than once, officiants made reference to RG3 (Robert Griffin, III), the now-famous Heisman Trophy winner, star quarterback of the Baylor Bears, and celebrated co-classmate. Proud parents, aunts, cousins, and friends whistled and hollered in celebration of their particular star's achievements. "Woo-hoo, way to go Darlene!" "You rock, Raj!" "AAAAAAAAArrrrrrrrrroooooooo! You did it, Amber!" It seemed that some had brought a cheering section of 30 or more! It was a near three-hour occasion filled with swells of emotion—beaming pride and joy, for the most part.

Graduation from college is a powerful moment—a celebration of lifelong learning and accomplishment. It is a time for those of us in the "supporting cast" to reflect on years of hoping, guiding, coaching, prodding, and praying. We look back all the way to the precious memory of sending them off to school for the very first time, then to their successive passages through elementary, middle, and high school. We ponder the challenges they faced, the successes they had, and the blooming of personal identity that happened over time.

Some of these memories are vividly etched in my mind. Even today, I can still sense the palpable emotion of August 21, 2007, bidding Audra adieu in the parking lot of the same Ferrell Center where we celebrated her graduation. We'd spent the day moving her in, decorating her dorm room at North Village, meeting her roomies, and doing the Wal-Mart run for toiletries and supplies. Her mother had, in my opinion, lollygagged throughout the day… stretching out those last few precious hours of togetherness. Eventually, it was time for the farewell, just before the Welcome Week Event scheduled at the basketball arena at 5 p.m.

We pulled into the parking lot. The three of us got out of the car. Toni holding Audra's hand. It was difficult to say much of anything at that point, I recall. With heavy sobs and heaving shoulders—and a look of uncertainty in her face—Audra could barely eke out "goodbye." A couple last hugs. "You can do this, Audra. God is with you. We love you." Her reply, with trembling lips, "I know. I'm just so sad right now." With our own emotions unhinged, choking back tears, we got into the car and were soon headed north on I-30. For the first hour or so, we drove along in silence, with only a few quiet tears, recognizing the power and the sacredness of that moment of life passage.

What struck me on graduation weekend, perhaps more powerfully than anything else, was that this was a time to affirm the truth that the deeply meaningful things in life take time—often many years. This is in contrast to so much of what we encounter day-to-day. Our society has an "instant gratification" mentality where expectations for immediate delivery of results have grown exponentially over the last few decades.

Whether its food, fame, sports, or work, Americans seem to crave instant results. We grow frustrated when our teams aren't winning, our career isn't fast-tracking, or our children aren't achieving what we "know" they are capable of. Our high-tech tools—while helping us do more with less than ever before—have also created a corresponding demand of immediate response and an expectation of "always being in touch." We're checking our smartphones during dinner, dangerously texting while driving, and surfing the net while wishing Mom happy birthday. This 21st century paradigm seems to me to be fostering an unhealthy mindset where we expect results in unrealistic time frames. It doesn't help that reality TV—think The Bachelor, Celebrity Apprentice, Biggest Loser, American Idol, and America's Next Top Model—reinforces the notion that romance, business success, weight loss, and instant celebrity can be achieved in the course of 8 or 10 weeks' elapsed time!

Yet most things worth having in life, such as solid relationships, an education, a close family, a successful business, a meaningful career—indeed, living out a fulfilling life purpose—tend to obey the "law of the farm." That is, there is a season of sowing and a season of reaping, and they are separated by time. And that time is almost always characterized by numerous nurturing efforts—and significant challenges—necessary to produce positive results. In fact, there is often a very long time that elapses between the time of sowing seed and ultimately bringing in the harvest. Usually, years. As microwave-mentality humans, though, that can be very frustrating!

Some business examples from my life, pieces of which I shared with you earlier, have proven the law of the farm to be very true.

iCyt comes to mind. We launched in late 2001 with a handful of folks. I figured to contribute my talents for a couple of years before replacing myself with a "permanent CEO." But two years became three, and then four, which turned to five and… well, you get the picture. We had to work through a lot of difficulty that included technology failures, contract ups and downs, fundraising travails, and moments of sheer terror when the very survival of the company was at stake. What is now celebrated as a success story of a prosperous start-up sold to Sony Corporation in late 2009 felt more like a high-octane theme-park ride for many years! I kept hoping for the ride to settle down, but instead, we seemed to pick up speed, endure more sheer drops, and take some hair-raising turns. In the words of the law of the farm, we kept sowing, kept watering, kept weeding, and kept fertilizing—all while warding off the rabbits and coyotes that threatened our existence. Eight years after launch, the harvest finally arrived.

Another example is the launch, the death, and the relaunch of my consulting firm, LifeVision, Inc. What in 1998 I thought would be more or less an instant success almost became my undoing as a business professional. By the time I experienced what seemed like my twenty-third failure in eighteen months (late 1999), I was ready to pack it in, buy a shovel and wheelbarrow, and go back to being a landscaper. Somehow, I had naively believed that my years of business training, my customer relationship skills, and my financial acumen would have paved the way to smooth sailing for LifeVision. The reality that I've since learned, however, is that few things in life are really "under our control" regardless of our talent, passion, and work ethic. With start-ups, there is always risk, and always the opportunity to fail. But if we can overcome the fear of a possible failure, there's always something to be learned in the process. By mid-2000, LifeVision was on life support, and a few years later it was essentially kaput. True to the law of the farm, however, some good root stock survived all of those winters—and when I left iCyt in 2008, the year before its sale to Sony, I was fortunate to be able to revive the company and relaunch it as Serra Ventures. Today, Serra is a thriving consultancy and entrepreneurial capital firm working with dozens of high-tech companies in the exciting milieu of the Research Park at the University of Illinois. What looked like a complete failure many years ago was actually the start of something beautiful, fruitful and sustainable. When I reflect on this, it reminds me that in the context of God's bigger story, we can take comfort that he is indeed in control. Each of us is uniquely hand-crafted by him to play an integral role in his story—whether succeeding or failing in the short run—and he will not let us down in the long run. That is our ultimate hope.

As these examples point out, "minding the gap" between sowing and reaping can be a real exercise in patience and perseverance—and trusting God. Fortunately, there are a number of strategies we can employ along the way:

1. **Hear what God is saying.**
   Each human being has been created with a unique combination of personality, talent, passion, and purpose. Likewise, each of our personal histories is one of a kind. We are, in this sense, irreplaceable. As I've said earlier, we each have a special role to play in God's bigger story. And as he invites us into his story, he's speaking to us. Through our circumstances, through scripture, through friends and family, perhaps in a dream, through a book or a sermon. He's providing the direction we need to align our little story with his big story, before we begin the process of sowing. Are we leaning in to listen?

2. **Take on the mindset of risk-taker.**
   I've shared a variety of stories in this book about taking risks. Some small, some quite outlandish, several in between. Taking on the mindset of risk-taker is important because it emboldens us to take the steps required to begin and continue the sowing process. I suppose it is human nature to prefer a zone of comfort and stability as opposed to taking risks. After all, if one takes a risk, there's always the chance of failure. But if you believe God is for you, that he is intimately acquainted with you and your story, and that he cares about you and your purpose (all of which is true!), then the prospect of failure isn't so frightening. Whether we succeed or fail isn't really the issue. When you put on the mindset of risk-taker, you become a ready instrument in God's hand.

3. **As you sow, envision the future.**
   The process of sowing—taking action toward fulfilling our purpose—is vitally important. Planting the seed on fertile soil and taking time to do it properly cannot be overemphasized. And while we sow, envisioning the future is important. In fact, a vision—an image—of what the potential future could be may be all we have to go on. With only a picture of our preferable future and no real proof that we can achieve it, the process of sowing represents the initial step in risking and making a commitment to create the new reality that we envision God has for us. We may not know what the future holds, but we can take heart that God has our back and is there to strengthen us throughout the journey.

4. **Expect and embrace setbacks.**
   You know that you'll encounter setbacks along the way. That's life. Having a posture of resilience during the growing season is the only way to make it through. The setbacks will require us to work hard on tending the growing crop. As I shared above, weeding, fertilizing, watering, and shooing away the varmints are all needed. But I suggest that we all go one step further—and that involves embracing the setbacks for what they can teach us, at least for a brief season. Value them for the lessons they convey—and then release them, setting your face forward.

5. **Focus on what you can impact.**
   Much—nay, most—of life is out of our control. We may not like that fact, but it's true. Contrary to the illusions we may want to believe, there is actually very little directly under our control. And that's okay. Focus on the immediate circle of influence that you have—your family, your team at work, your specific job assignment, etc.—and do the things you can do to make an impact in that circle. You won't accomplish much by spending time and energy on that which you don't control anyway.

6. **Nurture the positives.**
   As you browse the internet, watch TV, or read the newspaper, it won't take long to conclude that much of the news is negative. But to make progress on your journey, it's essential to weed out negativity, nurture the positives, and celebrate successes. Dwelling on bad news and allowing it to define your attitude and choices is a dead-end. As good things happen, take the time to celebrate the success and celebrate others who were involved in making it happen. Part of the "abundant life" promised us in the scriptures has to do with taking time to celebrate even small successes!

7. **Nourish and replenish your spirit.**
   The journey between sowing and reaping is a challenging one. And we'll naturally grow tired and have our strength sapped from time to time. So remember to rest your body, mind, and spirit. In particular, take the intentional steps to put your spirit in a position to be

replenished. Take time to be quiet, to meditate, to soak in the Spirit's presence, to saturate your mind with the scriptures. Take the time to offer your prayers to God, to allow him to comfort, refresh, and renew you.

8. **Keep God at the center.**

    Losing faith along the way is common because, let's face it, waiting and working isn't fun—especially when you put in strong efforts to see little to no results. But most of the time, this is how it works, with things unfolding more slowly and with more difficulty than we would like. It seems to be a hallmark of God's ways—and I suspect it's because he's as interested (more, maybe?) in our character development along the way as he is in our achievement of a specific result. Know that as you push ahead in faith, keeping God at the center and your personal identity firmly rooted in him, you will indeed see a harvest. Now, the harvest will probably look different than expected. Don't be disappointed. You may actually get to experience multiple harvests, so don't give up if the initial versions do indeed look different than you had hoped.

9. **Celebrate people!**

    Simply put, celebrate the people in your life, daily! Life is as much about the journey as it is the destination. Celebrate the reality that others are along with you for the ride. Love on them, hug them, and tell them how much you appreciate them.

10. **Embrace a life-long perspective.**

    And, finally, take comfort in the fact that some things will take a lifetime of growth—a lifetime of waiting between the initial sowing and the ultimate harvest. This is the way it is with many of the "bigger elements" of our personal stories. The most meaningful pieces of our life journeys will take their proper God-shape only with the considerable elapse of time—along with diligent work, prayer, and courage. So enjoy each part of the journey and don't be disillusioned if you haven't seen the expected results in just a few short months or even years. Embrace the truth that as we align with God's bigger story, he promises us a rich and abundant life along the way.

36. Touching God

San Diego, California
June 2012

I GRABBED MY BEACH CHAIR, BEACH BAG, WATER AND FLIP-FLOPS. My editor had just sent me a difficult email and I needed some time to noodle and pray about what he'd said. I tend to do that best by making an appointment with God at the beach. He typically shows up there.

As I walked along the boardwalk, I saw the usual delightful collection of bright umbrellas, families barbequing, couples playing hacky sack, teens boogie boarding, beach balls bouncing along, kids building sand castles. I also heard lots of laughter. The beach is a pretty joyful, vibrant, and colorful place. As I settled in just the right spot, I kicked off my sandals and wiggled my toes in the warm sand. I looked out on the waves crashing against the shore and the brilliant sun dancing on the ocean, and I began to reach out to and engage in a dialogue with the Creator.

"Tom wants me to consider turning the book into a memoir, instead of its present form as a collection of business anecdotes and advice. I don't know if I can do that. I'm not sure I know how to do that."

Silence. Waiting to hear from God during a time of prayer is often an exercise in quietness and patience. Two things I'm not very good at.

"The material in the book is good, but Tom says it could be much better. Is this the direction I'm supposed to go? I've been working on this for well over a year now. This new direction is likely to cost me another year of time. I'm just not sure."

A huge wave exploded in front of me—BOOM—salty spray everywhere. Beautiful.

Waiting.

Contemplating.

Allowing my spirit to quiet itself.

The rhythm of the water and waves was soothing.

The cadence was like a song.

I tuned my heart to listen.

Two thoughts came to me.

One, Tom has been in the editing and writing business for years. He knows what he's doing. I believed it was a God-thing to hire him several months ago. Why not trust him on this?

Two, good is often the enemy of great. I'd heard that phrase before, and I had seen it in action in several of the companies I'd worked with over the years. Though the book drafts were "good," perhaps they could be "great," or at least much better. That simple phrase began resonating with me.

As I processed these thoughts, a surge of courage welled up in me. In Christ, I had the requisite strength to do this. He would supply what I lacked in terms of talent and experience to put together a memoir. I needed to take the risk, heed Tom's advice, and do it. In that moment God was touching me in my beach chair. I was encountering Him firsthand, as I often had in times past.

Humans seem inexorably drawn to the ocean (and all kinds of bodies of water, actually). Families visit, routinely bring a picnic lunch, and stay the afternoon. Lovers come to stroll hand-in-hand, the waves lapping at their feet. Little children frolic along the shore, dancing in and out of the waves. Businesspeople pull to the side of the road, gazing at the rolling ocean, lost in thought. Whether stopping by on the way to work just to catch a 10-minute glimpse, coming for a half-hour jog, or sitting for an entire afternoon while reading a book, the ocean has an allure like no other.

It is a rarity in life when something captures our attention, our emotions, and our thoughts in an inexplicable and deep way. I know that I am personally drawn back again and again—both physically and in my spirit—to experience the invigoration and renewal offered me at the seashore, to visit with the Creator and receive his Spirit moving on me. As I have traveled back and forth between San Diego and Illinois for over 15 years, I've realized that one of the central reasons I am drawn to southern California is the profound moments I have experienced in connection with the Pacific Ocean. Moments of connecting with God, touching him. Each moment unique, powerful, potentially life-changing.

You often hear of the ocean mentioned as a source of inspiration, or perhaps as one of the primary reasons people move to a coastal city. But probing beyond the obvious, I'm intrigued why the ocean has this singular effect on some many. Just what is it about the ocean that so deeply stirs us, evoking a response like no other? One of the reasons is that a visit to the ocean provides us with a place of peaceful contemplation, particularly as we probe the meaning of our personal story and its connection to God's story at a deeper, reflective level.

But more than that, I believe that the ocean is the tangible representation of God and his nature—a place where we can touch him. That is its real power. So many aspects of God's nature are revealed through the ocean—abundance, power, hope, beauty, connectedness, permanence, mystery—to highlight just a handful. Visiting the ocean, in turn, connects us to these God-qualities, and to God himself, in a singularly unique way.

Abundance

If the ocean is anything, we know it is vast—abundant in so many ways. Covering three-quarters of the earth's surface, the ocean's breadth and depth defy human comprehension. When I visit the beach and view a small slice of the ocean's vastness, I am easily reminded of just how abundant and large God is. Way beyond me, yet intimately in relationship with me. Diverse beyond my understanding, yet reaching out to me. For me. Acquainted with my innermost thoughts.

The abundance of the ocean points me to God's generosity—his unlimited resources, always at the ready to meet the needs and desires of the humanity he created. In the presence of such generosity, I am challenged to be generous—to allow my life to be given away and my resources to be invested wisely. To become lavish in giving, so that I can experience what Jesus calls "real, abundant life."

Power

The ocean is power. What on one hand can be beautifully calm and accommodating can become on the other unleashed, ferocious, untamable power. And so I am pointed to God's power, as I look out on the rows of waves coming toward me. I am encouraged that his power is available to me, to enable me to accomplish that which I cannot do on my own. To intervene in situations that seem insurmountable. To catalyze the impossible. So much of life is encountering situations that are beyond our human ability to handle. Surrendering to God, allowing his power to be released into our circumstances and those we're in relationship with, is sometimes the only option that makes sense.

Hope

The ocean is the embodiment of hope. As I stand with waves lapping at my feet, the glint of the sun reflecting off the mica in the sand, I am encouraged with hope for something better than we are presently experiencing, hope for a world made right and whole. Through hope my imagination is stirred and my vision is enlarged. I'm able to think big thoughts and dream audacious dreams of creation in sync with the Creator—and people in right relationship with one another.

Without hope, my vision shrinks—and my actions align with that receding vision. I take fewer risks. I think self-centered and myopic thoughts. I am reduced to a shadow of what I am called to be. And so it is time well spent in a beach chair, book or newspaper in hand, a full afternoon of contemplation ahead of me. For there I am able to reconnect with and embrace new hope. I'm refreshed and energized with enlarged vision, and I am able to align my thinking with the larger truth outside of myself. I become emboldened to take new risks.

Beauty

Perhaps as important as any of its characteristics is the ocean's great, unparalleled beauty. When I have the occasion to watch the evening sun moving gently toward the horizon and the explosion of colors sweeping across the sky, I know that I am watching the earth's best, it's most majestic offering. And when I experience something that lovely, I cannot help but have my spirit deeply stirred. If God is anything, he is beauty. As a gift to us, he reveals that beauty through his constantly changing creation.

All of us need such moments wherein we can recalibrate, reset the lens through which we're viewing our life, our work, and our relationships. With so much that isn't beautiful in our world, beholding the ocean can adjust our view and illuminate that which has become obscured or hidden from us. Beauty can help me to believe again, to imagine the impossible as quite practical and indeed, achievable.

Connectedness

At a very practical level, the ocean represents the robust connectedness of the earth's ecosystems. The ocean's massive concentration of water provides temperature stabilization and cooling for the planet. The moon controls the rise and ebb of the tides. In a continuous cycle, the ocean receives water from rivers and streams, then has its water evaporated and subsequently delivered via rainfall to the land masses.

The ocean's connectedness, then, is a metaphor for the connectedness of each human to others, to the creation at large and to the Creator himself. Each of us represents an intricate and unique piece of something much greater. And what might not at first glance seem connected may in fact be connected. Our actions (and inactions) have a cause and effect, with seemingly miniscule exchanges between two people resulting in something profound or meaningful many years later or in ways they may not be aware of. As I embrace the truth that I am made in the Creator's image, I am challenged to also embrace the truth of my connectedness to each human being on the planet. Each made in his image. Each worthy of my respect and love.

Permanence

While the ocean is by definition always changing, moving, lively, and new, in another, broader sense it is permanent, stable, and eternal. In our breakneck-paced world, we need anchor points to which we can return time and again. Points that provide a landing place that is firm and unshakeable and permanent, a place to rest and rejuvenate.

The ocean is such an anchor point for me and one of the reasons I couldn't shake southern California from my memory when we moved back to Illinois in 1999. The ocean was one powerful magnet pulling me back to the Golden State with increasing frequency. The ocean represents permanence. It isn't going anywhere. God is permanent. He isn't going anywhere. And we can take solace in God's permanence, particularly when so many things in our lives are in constant motion and flux.

Mystery

Finally, the ocean is mysterious. It represents something unknowable, deep—so when we are drawn to the ocean we are drawn to something "beyond ourselves" and outside the boundaries of the known. From its vastness to the endless variety of plants and animals it contains to its ever-changing tidal movements, a visit to the ocean provides a tangible connection to something that it is otherwise ethereal. Spending time at the ocean affords us the opportunity to touch and contemplate the mysterious.

For many of us, particularly those passing into the latter half of our lives, the element of mystery becomes more of a friend and less of a threat. We understand that some conundrums in life aren't meant to be solved and that a certain measure of mystery is to be expected, perhaps even welcomed. Shades of gray become less daunting as we age (I guess our changing hair color helps us to accept gray more readily!). We discover that black-and-white answers aren't really appropriate for the biggest challenges we face. And we understand that as we move closer to "truth" in any given life circumstance, the more paradoxical it becomes. The ocean is symbolic of this mystery.

For me, then, the mystery of the ocean represents God in his bigness and his unknowable and eternal nature. It's at the seashore, looking out over the whitecaps and toward the horizon, that I am at once humbled, in touch with my smallness and his largeness, yet also lightened and cheered at the prospect of accepting the invitation He extends to all of humanity: to join him in the work of setting things right in the world.

37. God's Bigger Story (and How Yours Fits In!)

Anytown, Anywhere
August 2014

A MORE MEANINGFUL AND FULL LIFE IN THE PRESENT is most certainly the outcome of better understanding your personal story and acting in accordance with that understanding. As you better align your actions with a larger vision and purpose, more congruity occurs, and that, in turn, leads to a higher sense of satisfaction and significance. But even more, understanding where your story fits into God's Bigger Story can unleash real power—and lead to a truly abundant life. In this final chapter, I will switch gears a bit to talk about God's Bigger Story—the context in which each of our stories ultimately make sense.

God's Bigger Story, Part 1

In the very first chapter of the scriptures, we are told of God's most meaningful act of creation:

> God spoke: "Let us make human beings in our image, make them reflecting our nature so they can be responsible for the fish in the sea, the birds in the air, the cattle, and yes, *Earth* itself" (emphasis mine), and every animal that moves on the face of Earth." God created human be-

ings; he created them godlike, reflecting God's nature. He created them male and female. God blessed them: **"PROSPER! REPRODUCE! FILL EARTH! TAKE CHARGE!"** (Emphasis mine; Genesis 1:26-28, *The Message*).

These are power-packed bible verses, no doubt. It's what theologians refer to as the "creation mandate," and the good news is, it is still very much in play today. We can gather several pieces of insight from these words: one, we are literally made in the image of God, reflecting his very nature; two, we are in relationship with other humans as we can see from the plural form of "beings," and the use of the words "male and female"; and three, we are given a clear instruction to prosper, reproduce, fill the earth, and take charge of it. In Eden, we see a beautiful picture of humans tending and caring for God's creation, in harmony with him. In a very real sense, we see the pattern for being co-creators with him in fulfillment of the "take charge" part of the mandate. And over the centuries, we have seen limitless ways humans have become actively involved in the creation—through scientific discovery, the expansion of knowledge, the composition of art and music, the development of commerce, the establishment of government, and so on.

God's Bigger Story, Part 2

Of course, shortly after the giving of the creation mandate instruction, we see that humans disobeyed God in what theologians call "the Fall." The Fall corrupted, disrupted, and derailed humans in implementing all the elements of the creation mandate. Work became cursed. Relationships strained. Prosperity challenged. Some theologians go as far as saying that humans ceded to Satan their God-given mandate to take charge over the creation. And the result was, and in many ways still is, a mess.

But God had a plan to counter the Fall and its ugly ramifications. The scripture calls this plan God "setting things right." And he has been acting on this plan throughout the centuries. There are dozens and dozens of references using this, or very similar, phraseology throughout the scriptures, both Old and New Testaments. For example:

> ...He'll steadily and firmly set things right. He won't tire out and quit. He won't be stopped until he's finished his work—to set thing right on earth (Isaiah 42:1-4, *The Message*; the "He" refers to Jesus).

> They'll know I'm God when I set things right and reveal my holy presence (Ezekiel 28:20, *The Message*).

> You are right, O God, and you set things right (Jeremiah 12:1, *The Message*).

Much of the Old Testament is, in fact, a collection of stories, poems, prophecy, and history about humans either aligning with God's efforts to set things right, or on the other hand, ignoring, getting in the way of, or opposing God's plan.

God's Bigger Story, Part 3

While setting things right throughout the Old Testament, God drops several clues about his ultimate intention—that is, to establish his kingdom on the earth with the coming of the Messiah. And with these clues, he shows us the connectedness of the Messiah and his kingdom to the overall plan of setting things right. Two such references appear below:

> A new government of love will be established in the venerable David tradition. A Ruler you can depend upon will head this government, a Ruler passionate for justice, a Ruler quick to set things right. (Isaiah 16:5, *The Message*).

> When that time comes, I will make a fresh and true shoot sprout from the David-Tree. He will run this country honestly and fairly. He will set things right (Jeremiah 33:15, *The Message*).

Finally, it happened. Jesus appeared on the planet—and his life, ministry, death, and resurrection fundamentally changed the rules of the game. He came preaching and demonstrating the arrival of his kingdom on the earth, inviting all of humanity into relationship with him—and into fulfilling a vital piece of his Bigger Story. Two scriptures show the vital connection of Jesus to God's Bigger Story of setting things right:

> Jesus then appeared, arriving at the Jordan River from Galilee. He wanted John to baptize him. John objected, "I'm the one who needs to be baptized, not you!"

But Jesus insisted. "Do it. God's work, putting things right all these centuries, is coming together right now in this baptism" (Matthew 3:13-15, *The Message*).

The God-setting-things-right that we read about has become Jesus-setting-things-right for us (Romans 3:22, *The Message*).

So we see in the life and ministry of Jesus, indeed his bringing of the kingdom, the inauguration of a whole new meaning and experience of "setting things right." Essentially, through Jesus, the creation mandate to prosper and take charge is renewed, revitalized, and re-energized. Equally exciting is Jesus' invitation to each of us to join him! While I always thought this meant "be in relationship with him" (and it certainly does mean that), it means much more. That is, as we join ourselves to Jesus, we are invited into "joining the work he does," as the following scriptures point out:

> It's in Christ that we find out who we are and what we are living for. Long before we first heard of Christ and got our hopes up, he had his eye on us, had designs on us for glorious living, part of the overall purpose he is working out in everything and everyone. (Ephesians 1:11, 12, *The Message*).

> He creates each of us by Christ Jesus to join him in the work he does, the good work he has gotten ready for us to do, the work we had better be doing (Ephesians 2:10, *The Message*).

At the center of ourselves there is a being with a personal purpose, a story. Here we see that Jesus invites us to join our purpose, our story, with him and the "work he does." We have a most awesome invitation to join the grandest adventure of all time—to work with Jesus to "set things right" in the earth and throughout all of creation. In talking to many people over the last two decades, though, I've discovered that most have missed the more profound implications in all of this. Christians in particular tend to "spiritualize" these above scriptures and concepts. We interpret them to mean that through our daily Bible reading, praying, witnessing, and other spiritual activities, we fulfill the call of God to set things right. While this is true, it is only true in part. God has a much broader intent that is very practical—that we align our everyday, workaday lives to set some part of the creation "right"—whether by being an artist, a landscaper, a childcare worker, a parent, an inventor, a teacher, a scientist, or a shop owner.

God's Bigger Story, Part 4

Since the mid 1990s, I've been very encouraged and challenged by the writings of N.T. Wright, Dallas Willard, Eugene Peterson, Timothy Keller, Brian McLaren, and a handful of others. I consider these writers among the premier "thought leaders" in Christian theology and practice today. And most of them have explored, to one degree or another, the premise of life continuity beyond the grave, specifically the resurrected, re-embodied, physically constituted life that awaits us here on earth at the end of the age. And these writers have all highlighted that this is quite different from the disembodied, ethereal, heavenly form of eternal existence popularized in Christian writings over the last several hundred years.

In fact, this latter form of theology is the one in which I was raised—that we are here on earth for only a short time, in preparation for a heavenly existence, and that very little really matters in this present life beyond personal piety sufficient to get oneself through the door to the other side, if you will. I've discovered, however, that this is an incredibly shortsighted, narrow view—and one that tends to produce a certain set of behaviors and beliefs that run counter to living in a full, rich, and abundant way.

It has been my strongly growing conviction that our individual story and the deployment of our personal purpose will continue in a new, indeed more glorious, form on the other side of our physical death—and that this is the centerpiece to Part 4 of God's Bigger Story. In Part 4, Jesus returns to the earth to fully establish his kingdom here—"God moving into the neighborhood" as we see in the next-to-final chapter of the final book of the Bible, Revelation. In the eternal state of God's kingdom on earth, we join him in a resurrected, glorified bodily form that will have a variety of new attributes (looking forward to this, I must say!). We will have a body for a purpose—that is, there is much work yet to do, and we will do it in new, creative, presently inconceivable ways.

That which we put our hearts, hands, and minds to now, has the opportunity to be lasting and indeed foundational for eternity. This powerful truth has unlocked an entirely new way of looking at my story—and God's Bigger Story—in the present. It has made the discovery and execution of my personal purpose much more important. It has caused my interactions with others to take on entirely new meaning. It has opened up a universe of possibilities of "what might be." And, it has fundamentally altered how I approach living day-to-day, in the most practical and commonplace aspects of everyday life and relationships.

◆ ◆ ◆

Although it wasn't always so, I now see my personal story as intimately connected to God's Bigger Story—and it has become infinitely more meaningful because of that connection. And so it can be with your story. You have a personal story that has been written in part, is currently being written, and will continue to be written. And, you get the opportunity to participate in that writing at the invitation of the Creator, becoming a co-creator with him. As you take risks, big and small, and align your individual story with God's Bigger Story, you will enter in with him in his eternal work of setting all things right on the earth—and as a result, experience a profound richness to your life.

God bless!

Acknowledgements

Risking It took over three years to write, edit and publish. Along the way, a community of people was involved.

I'm grateful for the assistance of Alyssa, who prepared many of the initial chapter drafts from my notes. We had thought about working on a book project together for several years, so it was wonderful to actually do it!

Many thanks to Tom Hanlon who was a godsend in the middle of the process. Tom prodded me toward a memoir when I didn't have a real firm grip on what it would consist of. Thanks, Tom, for doing that—but even more for your excellent editing work!

To the Serra team that supported the effort—Dennis Beard, Eric Wilson, Rob Schultz and David Hodge—thanks for hanging with me for the length of time it took to get to the finish line!

To the team of people that took time to read the manuscript draft and send comments, thank you.

To my brother Ben, though our Tuesday morning coffee breaks have become less frequent (and are now on Saturdays half way between our two cities), thanks for encouraging me to continue towards the vision of being a writer and speaker.

And to Toni, my number one cheerleader and encourager for over 30 years. You have been the most loving, helpful and supportive person in my life—and this story is just as much yours as mine. Love you forever!

About the Authors

Tim Hoerr: Tim is the CEO of Serra Ventures, LLC, a professional services firm offering assistance in business strategy, capital formation, and organization development. He is the Managing Partner of Serra Capital which provides funding to seed, emerging and growth stage funding to high tech companies in selected sectors. Tim is also the Managing Member of The Best Sammich I Ever Had, a Jimmy John's franchisee operating in central Texas.

Tim was formerly a partner in the international accounting and consulting firm, RSM McGladrey, in Illinois and San Diego. He spent nearly 15 years with the Firm. In the 2000's, Tim served as President of SourceGear, a software firm, and then as Co-Founder and Chief Executive Officer of iCyt, a bioscience instrument firm which won numerous technology and business awards. The company was acquired by Sony Corporation in 2009. He won the Entrepreneurial Excellence in Management Award at the Innovation Celebration in 2009.

Tim previously authored the book Thank God It's Monday! A Toolkit for Aligning Your Lifevision and Your Work. For over 30 years in business, Tim has actively sought to integrate his understanding of God's kingdom into every aspect of his life, including all of his business endeavors. He enjoys the challenges of wrestling with and applying faith principles in the marketplace. Perhaps most importantly, he is excited to share his successes and failures with the businesspeople and entrepreneurs who are building today's high performance organizations.

Alyssa Kolb: Alyssa is the Marketing and Communications Director for Serra Ventures. A graduate from the University of Illinois at Urbana-Champaign (undergrad) and the Chicago School of Professional Psychology (masters), she has extensive training and background in the field of Industrial Organizational Psychology, essentially how human factors influence people's behavior and interactions within organizations.

Alyssa has performed a variety of functions for Serra Ventures since joining the firm in 2009. In addition to working on client projects, she prepares and distributes the Serra Capital Quarterly Newsletter, maintains and updates the Serra Ventures website, and prepares all workshop and speaking presentation materials for Serra Ventures. She has also authored numerous white papers covering topics in entrepreneurship and start-up ventures. She is the oldest of Tim's three daughters.

To contact Tim for a speaking engagement or related matters:
tim@serraventures.com
217.819.5201
www.timhoerr.com
www.serraventures.com

Serra Ventures, LLC
2021 South First Street, Suite 206
Champaign, IL 61820

www.ingramcontent.com/pod-product-compliance
Lightning Source LLC
Chambersburg PA
CBHW071451040426
42444CB00008B/1296